Happy reading
Carol Gregson

Leaky Boots

and other complaints

Written and illustrated by

Carol Gregson
aka the Pottersville Complainer

I

Leaky Boots

And other complaints

Written and illustrated by

Carol Gregson

aka The Pottersville Complainer

Printed and bound in the United States of America

ISBN# 0-9742031-0-6

First printing 2003

Design and composition by Kent Gregson

For information; write Carol Gregson

1116 county route 29, Olmstedville, NY,12857

Publishing a book is a little like childbirth: a lengthy process with lots of assistance. This process was begun at the Academy for Learning in Retirement at Saratoga Springs, with assistance of its writers group, headed by Marianne Finnegan and assisted by Marion Renning. The manuscript was edited by Bette Ann Moskowitz and later re-edited by Alice Gilborn, who also graciously wrote the fore-word. Final book design was done by #3 son, Kent Gregson, and #1 daughter, Kris Moss, handled detail management. My good friend, Fran Gamble, is responsible for that Pottersville Complainer title. It's been mostly fun.

Credit for all this material, though, goes to my seven children, Kris, Eric, Barry, Kent, Blair, Jill and Lance, and their father, Greg, who was responsible for the whole thing. I love them all.

CONTENTS

FOREWORD

You may be one of those people whose personal geography does not include New York's Adirondack Mountains. Even downstate New Yorkers—meaning those in The City—can register confusion at the mention of any place north of Westchester County, as Carol Gregson aptly points out in her chapter "Nowhere." Early cartographers had their own problems with this huge sweep of mountains, lakes and forest snuggled up to what is now the Canadian border, calling it unfit for cultivation, a "dismal wilderness" better to be avoided. Lucky for us several centuries later that Gregson and a few thousand other enterprising individuals chose not to avoid it but to spend their lives in it, cultivating it according to their needs.

The region is one of contrasts, home to frigid winters and fecund summers, gorgeous vistas and decadent swamps, black bears and flies, hermits and churchgoers, the idle rich and the working poor. In the last few hundred years it has tolerated hunters, sportsmen, landholders, entrepreneurs, vacationers, environmentalists, artists—and writers who have succeeded in varying degrees in mining its potential for comedy and tragedy. In the nineteenth century, Philander Deming's short stories captured its menacing gloom; in the twentieth, a bevy of poets and wilderness lovers trumpeted its natural and spiritual beauty. In the twenty-first century, Carol Gregson offers us still another perspective—the sheer humor of getting on with life in a place where life is not always easy.

The forty-four very short stories in *Leaky Boots* cover over half a century (less "six years of fruitless wandering") from 1945 when Carol arrived in the Adirondacks from Seattle, a young bride and pregnant, to the present. During this time she and her husband Greg, a forester, produced seven children (five boys and two girls) and a book full of delightful complications with Carol at the center. Although she eventually became an art teacher, she is naturally a storyteller, reaping the comic implications of her own, unexaggerated experiences. She writes in a simple, straightforward way, addressing her readers and sometimes even asking our opinion before delivering her own with deadpan irony. One suspects that when she first saw how puny the Adirondacks looked next to the Cascades, the stage was set.

Most of us can identify with Carol's subjects—building a house by bits and pieces, a Fourth of July fireworks gone awry, coping with wayward goats and children, or trying to wrestle a couch through a new door. Other stories have a decided Adirondack flavor like digging ginseng or trapping a bear at the family run campsite in Schroon Lake. Some of her best passages have to do with her boys, son no. 1, 2, 3, etc., as she prefers to call them. Speaking from experience, in "Vroom, Vroom" she speculates on what appeals to men: "Being of the female persuasion, I'm not sure what comes first in the hearts of men: whether it's hunting, fishing, contact sports, war maneuvers, speed or rearranging the landscape. I have had occasion, however, to notice the happy preoccupation of the male of the species with heavy machinery. It must be the feeling of power." Describing her husband's pride at replacing the logging horse with a bulldozer, she says, with resignation, "It looked so small to me. And the payments looked so large."

"Virtual is a Seven Letter Dirty Word," enumerates her struggles to come to grips with a computer, a nearly universal experience for anyone over fifty. "Minority Report" has a ring of hard truth when she writes about the persistent poverty of the region. "They [newcomers who have recently 'discovered' the Adirondacks] will mention unpainted houses, porches full of discarded machinery and yards strewn with old abandoned vehicles. They will ask why the locals don't clean up their act, instead of besmirching nature's glory. They might even go so far as to say that we who live here don't appreciate what we have." Her explanation, not to be construed as an apology, is too long to quote here but can be summed up in one sentence: "To begin with, one cannot eat the scenery."

Carol Gregson calls herself "The Pottersville Complainer." Hers are complaints anyone will be happy to hear. As Gregson brushes life's little problems with her dry wit, adding her own line drawings just to make sure we get the point, we see the Adirondacks in a kinder, brighter light. *Leaky Boots* makes me glad I lived there twenty-eight years. I had no idea what I was missing.

Alice Wolf Gilborn
Founder, *Blueline Magazine*

COMING TO THE ADIRONDACKS

My Aunt Emily warned me. "Before you marry that young man," she said, "make sure he has indoor plumbing."

I knew, of course, that there were some people somewhere in the world who still used outhouses. But this was 1945. My sailor was from New York State. Everybody knew that New York was the center of all things progressive. I mean, if you're from a place like Seattle, where everything is pretty casual, you know for sure that plumbing, electricity, high heels and sophistication are alive and well in New York. I'd seen all the movies.

It was true, of course, that he'd talked a lot about his Adirondack Mountains. He'd kept whole busloads of us civilians entertained with his tales of bears and skunks, loons and bats, deer, snow and cold. But it all sounded great to me. Love is completely blind.

When the war was finally over, we arrived home to his beloved Adirondacks on the first day of hunting season. It was not an auspicious beginning. I was so busy with morning sickness, we almost missed the stop at the Albany train station where we took the bus north. I found that his mountains were certainly wild and untidy, but they were not very high, and

1

though there was a lot of rock, the trees kept right on growing clear up and over the tops. I was used to a more vertical landscape. On the other hand, I had not actually lived in the middle of it.

As the bus lumbered northward, I watched for historic sites. Westerners always look for history when they come east. We always figure that everybody has more history than we do. Instead, I was seeing trees. They were not the large stately ones that I was used to. They were smaller. But there were lots of them.

Then, every few miles I noticed there were clusters of little box-like buildings which turned out to be old motels, or "bungalows," most of which seemed to be abandoned. Greg explained it was the "off season." It looked to me as though the off season had been that way since the start of the war. Gazing out the window as we approached our destination, I noticed a strange looking cement structure among the trees which looked like it might have been meant for somebody's basement, except there were no doors or windows. Small trees were growing inside it.

"What's that?" I asked. "Oh, that's just where some fellow thought he'd put a swimming pool. That's as far as he ever got. Probably ran out of money. Don't think he ever figured out how to make it hold water, anyway."

A bit farther on, we passed what looked like a little platform, out there in the woods, with a lonely looking kitchen chair sitting in the middle of it.

"What's that?" I asked.

"Oh, that's left over from the big hurricane that blew through here in 1936."

Curiouser and curiouser. Seemed to me that people ought to clean up after themselves.

The little town where his father met the bus did not even qualify for a stoplight, and their house was three miles away, down a dirt road.

His parents' home had been built during the war, with all its shortages. There was still (you guessed it!) an out-house. For the same reason, my mother-in-law was cooking on a coal-burning kitchen stove. She kept it polished, and cooked amazing meals on it. I was completely overwhelmed.

Her reaction to her son's new bride was somewhat similar. It was obvious that I was not going to be a handy addition to her household. I was young, pregnant and inept. We more or less circled each other.

Did I mention the heating system? There was no furnace yet. The house was heated with a fireplace and a kerosene heater. Our bedroom, up under the eaves, was not heated at all, and I was more appreciative than ever of my husband's warm body at night. Also, since I had never experienced temperatures lower than about seventeen degrees, I became fascinated with the readings. They soon became a lot lower than seventeen degrees.

It was in this manner that I was introduced to life in the Adirondacks. As the winter wore on, and my waistline expanded with our first child, I learned to curtail my trips to that outhouse. I learned how to take a bath with about two quarts of water, but I never did get the hang of cooking on that stove. The fact is, I never got near it. It was just as well. Those dampers were beyond my understanding.

The snow got higher, and the temperature kept getting lower. I wrote to my mother in early February and said, "It's three degrees below zero outside, and it's noon. What do you think?" She wrote back saying, "Isn't it wonderful that you are young and healthy and able to adjust to changes?" which freely translated meant, "You asked for it. Quit complaining."

Now, many years later, I can tell that I am a real Adirondacker. When my western relatives tell me that my breathtakingly beautiful Adirondack pictures look like "pretty good second or third growth timber," I get indignant. We raised seven natives here, and our grandchildren are second-generation, busily overrunning these hills. I naturally wear boots from October to April, and measure distances in terms of hours on the road rather than city blocks. I have been stuck in deep mudholes on roads that are now paved, and I can tell you about navigating a road up near Paradox called Stony Lonesome that is stony and lonesome, but definitely not a road. Heavy traffic makes me nervous, but I can handle the snow.

I usually forget to lock my door, and it's probably a good thing because the chances are that I won't remember where the key is. These mountains are as high as I want to climb, and some have blueberries on top. I can borrow a canoe and a clutch of grandchildren and get lost for an after-noon, and then come home for a fireside chat. I still like to remind people on a cold and rainy October day that this is mid-winter weather where I come from, but nobody pays any attention. They're used to me.

THE DISEASE

Adirondack is the name of a disease. Something on
the order of diabetes, perhaps. It's a condition you might not
die of, although the complications thereof might do you in,
but it's a thing you have to learn to live with and make adjust-
ments for. And it shapes your character. It really does.

The odd thing about this malady is the way it creeps
up on you. I will admit Greg had me distracted, but there
were very few clues. The scenery was certainly pleasant. It
was fall. The trees were disarmingly brilliant. The sky was
amazingly blue. The weather was, well, exhilarating.

Then gradually it began to get colder. Pretty soon it
was cold enough to qualify as mid winter where I came from.
The trouble was, it was only late October. That was when I
began to notice how very few houses had central heating.
There were wood stoves and kerosene stoves and coal stoves
and gas heaters and fireplaces. They all seemed to need a lot
of attention. In some houses there were some rooms that were
simply closed off in the winter. People seemed to just sort of
condense themselves. I hesitate to use the word, hibernate. It
was all so primitive.

It kept right on getting colder, and I kept watching the
thermometer drop with fascinated horror. And then it snowed.

That was a whole other complication. If you had not covered your woodpile, now you had to dig down through the snow to it. There was the tedious ritual of putting on and taking off layers of underwear, jackets and coats, scarves, gloves, mittens, hats, socks and boots. No combination was ever quite enough, and no group of hooks or furniture was ever sufficient to hold all the drying items when you came inside. Also, inside, you could never be warm on both sides at the same time. Except in bed—if you remembered to heat it first with a hot brick.

Finally I began to notice that everyone's car was covered with snow, or encased in ice. That's when I realized how few garages there were. The world was quite solidly stocked with jumper cables, and it was necessary to park judiciously at night to minimize the shoveling and pushing and shoving in the morning.

So much for winter. I watched in amazement and waited for spring. Well, it was late. While mother wrote about daffodils, we were still languishing under all that snow. About the time she was talking rhododendrons, an amazing new event was taking place in the Adirondacks. It's called mud season. All that ice and snow turned to muck. Boots that tried to be warm all winter turned out not to be waterproof in the spring. The roads became fascinating mine fields full of dark holes into which car tires would sink. The challenge was to keep your wheels on the ridges between the bottomless ruts, and never to pause in your forward momentum for fear you would settle in permanently. The skillful driver would rock his car gently from reverse to second gear and back in order to persuade it out of some muddy grave. Drivers who raced their motors and spun their wheels would dig themselves ever deeper into the mire, and subject themselves to the derision of rescue crews with bulldozers and come-alongs. A comealong is a contraption of ropes and pulleys that hitches to a tree or some other handy thing to get you out of trouble. These were not gravel roads. They were dirt roads. The Adirondack geology seems also to be a mixture of extremes. You are either on bedrock, or else in the muck.

When mud season finally subsided and rhubarb was on everybody's menu, there was yet another Adirondack surprise. It's called the black fly. Just when everyone was ready to plant a garden, just when the temperature rose into the temperate zone and apple trees were blossoming, and you could venture outside again without a heavy jacket, those little black specs would descend upon you in clouds, driving you right back inside. Children would come in from play with blood streaming from behind their ears. Determined fishermen would appear in wide brimmed hats draped in nets, decorated with fairly solid patterns of black flies looking for their pound of flesh. No inch of exposed skin was safe from these varmints. Their bite is vicious, the itch is intense, and the welts last for days. Not until the fourth of July is anyone safe from their deadly attack.

Through all this the true Adirondacker perseveres.

That's the way it is with this disease. He will say, "Bugs? What bugs?" He will chuckle about the flatlander who disregards the "road closed" sign, and needs to be extracted from a muddy grave. He will breathe deeply of the frosty air, and eat "trail stew" at hunting season when the buck evades him. While he cuts and stacks his firewood, he'll plan, someday, to put in a furnace. He'll make gallons of maple syrup while talking about putting up a garage—someday—so he won't have to keep shoveling the snow out of his pickup truck. But first he's going fishing. It's the nature of the disease.

POTTERSVILLE COMPLAINER

For those of you who don't live in New York State, it's time for a little lesson on the political divisions here. I don't know who invented the system, or where it all began, but I think maybe it's from the dark ages. Here's how it works. Every county is divided up into townships, and these townships are actually territories that make up each county. They don't necessarily have much to do with the actual town you might encounter. Apparently "town" is a relative term.

For instance, Brant Lake is a little village in the township of Horicon. It is located at the southern end of the lovely, five mile long Brant Lake. Also included in the Horicon township is the town of Adirondack, which is even smaller than the village of Brant Lake, and is located on the eastern shore of Schroon Lake. Both of these towns are so small that the Adirondack Park Agency refers to them as hamlets. Every time I hear that term I am reminded of the Pied Piper of Hamlin, and as soon as I put that thought out of my mind, I start thinking of hamsters. For some reason, I can't get serious about anything called a hamlet. It sounds like a baby pig.

Right now I live in a little place called Olmstedville, which is a part of the Town of Minerva. There is also a little community called Minerva which shares this township. It's hard to tell which is smaller, but the Minerva School is in Olmstedville. It has about 150 students, K through 12. That's the best we can do. I don't know how this all works out in the large cities of New York State, and I really don't want to know. I'm happier this way.

So now that you understand all that, let me tell you about the Town of Chester. It is mainly made up of Chestertown and Pottersville. Chestertown is a pretty good sized town for these parts. It even has a supermarket and a drug store, and a movie theatre which is open during the summer.

Pottersville is smaller. There was a time when the Wells House there was an overnight stop for summer people on their way to various places on Schroon Lake. People used to come by train to the station in Riparius, which is a part of the Town of Johnsburg. Then they'd take a stagecoach across the bridge over the Hudson River and go through Riverside, which is another little part of the Town of Chester. The stage-coach would follow the shore of Loon Lake to Pottersville and they would stay at the Wells House overnight. Then they'd go on a mile or so to the steamboat landing at the southern end of Schroon Lake and be on their way. They'd stay all summer. All that was back in the late 1800's, early 1900's—before my time. My grandchildren find it hard to believe that anything was before my time.

When I met up with Pottersville, in 1945, the Wells

House was still operating under the watchful eyes of Maurice and Leila O'Connell. We attended the alumni dinner for the Pottersville High School Class of 1942, and my new husband made a speech. I don't remember a thing he said, but it must have lasted at least one and one half minutes. I was busy trying not to notice how gorgeous his old girlfriends were.

These days the Wells House is headquarters for a vast number of motorcyclists, and I don't think I'd fit in very well. Pottersville is now mostly the site of a busy truck stop known as the Black Bear. The superhighway we call the Northway that connects Albany and Montreal has a convenient exit there. Once there was a real stuffed bear standing outside the door of the Black Bear, but I think it succumbed to the weather. Now there is a big sign depicting a few bears sitting on stools. I really enjoy that sign. The old general store has closed and is for sale. The school is abandoned. There's a garage and an auto-parts store, and a hardware store, and three or four little churches. That's about it.

I've heard that there used to be a big Pottersville Fairgrounds that everyone for miles around went to, but that was also before my time. The dance hall called the Glendale where I learned to square dance was left over from that, I think, but it is also gone.

I have a very good friend who lives in Pottersville, and when I started to regale her with all these complaints I have about the Adirondacks, she decided I might just as well extend my remarks to a wider audience. Maybe she was hoping it would wear me out. So she got me booked to speak to the Chestertown Historical Society, and we decided to call me the chronic complainer. That was all right with me. I enjoy complaining. Her mistake was to try to get the whole thing publized. She called a local paper with all the information, but they somehow got it garbled, and I was billed as the Pottersville complainer.

This also didn't bother me. I'd just as soon be a Pottersville complainer as an Olmstedville complainer. But she's upset. She says I've never lived in Pottersville, so I have no right to complain about it. I'm not sure why this is such an issue with her. She's actually from Boston, and has only lived in Pottersville for 40 years or so. You should hear her accent!

So I figure I'll go right on being the Pottersville complainer. I just happen to live 5 miles farther out in the woods in Olmstedville. Now if you want me to come and complain at your place, just call my agent. She lives right there in beautiful downtown Pottersville. Pay no attention to her sputtering.

A PLACE CALLED CHESTERTOWN

You may have noticed by now that I am not a native Adirondacker. I've only lived in these parts for about 50 years. But six of my children were born in Ticonderoga, so I make my claim by proxy through them. The seventh child was born in Warsaw—not Poland—out near Buffalo, in Wyoming County. But he did all his school years in Schroon Lake, so I reckon some day he'll qualify—or maybe his grandchildren.

I was born and raised in a small town near Seattle in the state of Washington. The whole west coast is not California, and Seattle is not in Oregon. This Washington is not a city in the District of Columbia; it's a state in the Pacific Northwest. I'm not trying to be facetious—just making sure there's no confusion.

The Seattle region is a place where the norm is moderation in all things. The climate is moderate. Not too hot in summer, and not too cold in winter. Out there, the rain coming in off the Pacific dumps mostly on the rain forest of the Olympic Peninsula, and then Seattle gets the rest when the clouds bump up against the Cascade Mountains. It doesn't beat down with thunder and lightning; it falls gently, like a line from Shakespeare. And the Japanese current keeps it warm. In the summer, windows are left open without screens, because there are not a lot of insects. It may snow a few inches in February, but you have to get out and slide fast, because it doesn't last. The thing to wear in Seattle is maybe a suit. In winter you put on a raincoat over it, and in summer you take off the jacket.

Seattle people tend not to get too excited about things. It just isn't necessary. And everybody keeps the car in the garage, although the boat and trailer might have to stay outside. And there is central heating. The world is sensible and neat, and Mount Rainier presides over the whole thing.

So I met this sailor, who said he was from the Adirondacks in New York State. I thought this sounded interesting. Visions of Sleepy Hollow and Rip Van Winkle and Ichabod Crane surfaced in my mind. I didn't know I had the wrong mountains until later. And he talked funny. Mother called it a brogue. It turned out to be a Long Island accent. He was not a native of these parts either. But I didn't discover he'd lived anywhere but the Adirondacks until after I married him. He didn't think it was important.

The Town of Chester is where we first settled. Chestertown is a small town in the Adirondack Mountains of New York State. For those of you who have never been to New York, an explanation is in order. First of all, New York is not completely paved. New York City is confined mostly to a small island at the end of the Hudson River called

Manhattan. This island is mostly made of bedrock, which is a good thing, because the place sees lots of heavy use. The rest of New York State is very large, and a lot of it is rural. Chestertown is not just "upstate." That term usually means Albany or Syracuse or Rochester or Buffalo. We're talking North Country now, and the emphasis is on rural. Also, it's inside an imaginary line called the Blue Line, which refers to the boundary of the Adirondack Park. This is a rather unusual kind of park. For one thing, it's big—the biggest state park in the United States. About the size of the state of Vermont. Those of us who live here get to wondering every now and then how it would be to have our own state. Then nobody else would be telling us what we can or can't do. I bet we could even call up our governor and have a chat. After all, there are only about 150,000 of us.

Another unique feature is the fact that about half of this big park is privately owned. The big paper corporations own lots of it, and a lot of it is owned by little people like me. So we have these small towns, and one of them is Chestertown. These little towns are like little city-states, and the rivalry between them is keen. There is so much territory between them, there is not a lot of togetherness. This leads to interesting battles on the basketball courts, among other things.

I met up with Chestertown in 1945, at the end of World War II. The Rising House was still a working hotel then, but the Chester House was soon torn down. Archie

Meade had a general store next to the bank, and Beecher
Jones ran a unique taxi service from a booth just outside. The
A&P was on Church Street right around the corner from
Janser's Drug Store, and there was a meat market next door.
Mark and Caroline Fish ran the mercantile store on the other
corner, and Itso Sumi's photography studio was just up the
street. Dr. Blodgett's office was on Theriot Avenue, and he
lived upstairs. That was when doctors still made house calls.
Down near Faxon's Pond was the veneer factory, where the
tannery used to be, and next to the Episcopal Church was a
big two-story building that used to be a glove factory, after it
had been a school.

In 1948 we bought about 75 acres out where Theriot
Avenue joined up with Route 8. We bought it from Mrs.
Brown, who lived in a charming home next to Fish's store.
There had been a sawmill on the property we bought, and
there were piles of slab wood all over the hill where we
intended to build our house. I think we paid Mrs. Brown
$1200 for the place. We worried that she might die before we
finalized the sale, but she lived on a number of years afterward. Everybody looks old when you're in your 20s. She was
a charming lady, and had us in for tea while we negotiated.

We had visions of building a modern modular home
there. We were strongly influenced by Frank Lloyd Wright.
But first we had to house our menagerie of goats, pigeons,
rabbits, dogs and cats. So while we did that, we pitched a big
army tent down by the brook, where we planned to spend the

summer. We were full of confidence. We would do it our-selves, and pay as we went. Which meant that our house did not progress very quickly. I learned how to mix cement that summer and did some fairly good laying of cement blocks, but I was forever taking time off to look after our two year old or feed the rabbits, and Greg kept having to take time off to earn some sort of living for us. Tent living was pretty informal and easy going in the summer, but we were still there in October, and it was getting cold. I'm not very good company when I'm cold. Hunting season was fast approaching, and we didn't have the roof on yet.

Mrs. Warner had been telling me that if my ears were any good I certainly wouldn't be living in that tent. But wild animals didn't worry me—I was too cold. We finally got to the shingling, and it took us three or four beautiful fall days. After that, we moved into three rooms, and Greg went hunt-ing. I got to sleep in a real house again, with walls and win-dows, and even a little heat. It was good to settle in and rest my sore knees.

There was still no running water, or electricity, but we had a kerosene space heater. It seemed as though everything we needed in those days cost another $50 which we didn't seem to have. It was a good thing we were young and healthy. Mother kept reminding me.

One day a vacuum cleaner salesman found us. I could not believe it. Our walls were not finished. We had only a sub floor, and this salesman wanted to sell us a vacuum cleaner. I kept telling him it was no use, but he was determined. He decided to give me a demonstration, and got the thing all ready to go before I remembered we had no electricity. That did it. He was out of there in a flash.

I was cooking on a gas hotplate, with a top-of-the-stove oven. Greg and his father had finished up their seasonal produce business with bushels of leftover fruit and vegetables. There was a lot of butternut squash, which I made into pumpkin pies. I discovered that my mother's recipe for pumpkin pie was not only delicious, but also foolproof. I could mix it up and put two pies in that oven and go take a nap. Whenever I woke up, those pies were just right. You should ask me for my recipe sometime.

At Christmas it made pretty good shortbread, too. We were still hammering away, and the Christmas tree kept falling over, but the view from our hilltop was a pleasant one, and Chestertown was turning out to be not too bad, after all.

THE BIG BANG

When I was a kid, the Fourth of July always commenced at dawn with a loud explosion. Independence Day! Wow! My two big brothers put a giant firecracker under a great big empty tin can and set it off in our driveway.

It was a royal sendoff to a magnificent day! In the morning there was a big parade, which wound up at the city park where there were games of all kinds and plenty of hot dogs and ice cream. All the boys kept us girls busy dodging cherry bombs. If you didn't need to dodge a lot of them, you just weren't very popular.

The finish line for the boat race down the Cedar River was right there at the park. It was a seven-mile race down from Maple Valley and the river was pretty shallow in places. The contestants had to get out of their boats sometimes and drag them across sand bars. Sometimes that put a few holes in their hulls. There were always a few fellows coming across the finish line, paddling like mad, in a boat which was entirely under water.

When darkness finally came, we went home and ran around with sparklers while Daddy and the boys set off roman candles. There were others blasting off all over town. We all loved the huge celebration that was the Fourth of July. Every year.

Then, the Japanese bombed Pearl Harbor, and everything changed. For the next four years we fought World War II. Nobody had the time, the inclination, or even the ammunition to celebrate Independence Day. There were plenty of explosions going off all over the world.

By the time all that was over, I was not a kid any more. I was a grown up married lady with a new baby, living three thousand miles away from where I started out. It was the same great country, though, and there was a lot more to celebrate. I looked forward to seeing how it was done in the Adirondacks. I was not disappointed.

Even in the small towns among these hills, there were still parades and speeches and fun, but there was a new respect for fireworks. On the night of the Fourth of July, the firework displays were left to the experts. We could all recount stories of kids who had been maimed or blinded by the misuse of fireworks, and besides, the war had sent home a good many badly wounded men. Our local fire departments took over those duties and everybody was pretty comfortable with that.

I think the best firework display I ever witnessed was some time in the mid fifties at the millpond in Brant Lake. We had three or four children by then. We loaded them into the car and went over there and parked by the side of the pond with all the other folks for miles around. The millpond is right in the middle of town, and there's a nice big stone fountain out in the middle of it, like a little island. The firemen had situated their material out there all ready to go off in proper sequence. When it got dark enough, they rowed out there in two or three boats, smoking their cigars, getting ready to start the show.

Then one of them dropped his cigar. In the wrong place. At the wrong time. Suddenly, everything went off all at once. There were multiple explosions. Streaks of light flew off in all directions. The bombs were bursting in air with wild abandon. It was a glorious sound and light show! The really greatest sight, though, was watching all those men, silhouetted against all that light, diving into the water and swimming for shore.

It was, as I said, the most impressive display of fireworks I think I have ever personally experienced. We all tooted our horns with great enthusiasm, and went home happy. Since then I've seen some magnificent and well organized displays, louder and brighter, and longer lasting. But the one I will always remember is that amazingly beautiful Brant Lake fiasco.

The Big Bang!

WHO'S THE GOAT?

The man I married was an enthusiastic kind of fellow. That was one of the many reasons why I liked him. I don't think I quite understood, though, the extent to which his enthusiasms would go, or their various directions.

It was predictable that we should have a cat, and that kittens would follow. And you would, of course, expect a dog, and then puppies. Then, when he was working at the mouse farm (where laboratory animals were raised) they were experimenting with rabbits. When the experiments didn't work out, we acquired some nice New Zealand Red rabbits.

After that there was a flock of racing pigeons. At one time the local resorts each had a flock of pigeons, and they held races during the season, but that practice had faded at about the time that World War II had come along. Somehow, we acquired the last flock. It came with its own coop. He simply could not refuse.

And finally, of course, there were the goats. Greg's father was allergic to cow's milk, so his parents bought two Toggenburg goats from somewhere on Long Island. Of course, goats need to be bred in order to produce milk, and then there are those goat kids. If you have ever seen a kid goat romping around, you don't need to be told what enticing little animals they are. Their joy in simply being alive is infectious. So very soon we had goats. Toggenburg goats are especially attractive. They look a lot like deer. And they are very intelligent. This may or may not be an asset. It depends on your point of view. My point of view was not the same as Greg's. He had great fun playing hide and seek with them and chasing around. I get nervous around animals that I suspect are smarter than I am. Besides, I was outnumbered. These goats soon tired of our one acre, and decided to pull up stakes (literally), and case the neighborhood. They were particularly fond of the neighbor's roses. Relations with the neighbors soon became strained.

It was bad enough having to chase after rabbits when our two-year-old decided to open their hutch and climb in with them, but having to herd wayward goats as well was beginning to wear.

So we did the sensible thing. We sold our neat little house with its one little acre, and bought some larger acreage so that our burgeoning herd could have more suitable room.

The first thing we built there was the goat house, and a fenced in area larger than our one acre had been. It even had a brook running through it. What more could any goat wish for? There were also numerous rabbit hutches, since our rabbits had been fruitful and multiplied. An old army tent served as living quarters for us until we got our house built.

So did our goats live happily ever after? Well, no. They

considered that fence a challenge. Their morning patrol would pace that fence looking for a weak spot. When they found one, they would put the smaller kids to work nosing under any little hole they could make. Then they would work their way up to the larger ones until there was a hole large enough for the whole herd to be off exploring their new world. It didn't happen every day—just often enough to keep us on our toes. One morning we awoke in our tent to find the entire herd filing solemnly through. I did not panic. I merely dived under the covers and stayed there until the man of the tent had taken care of the situation.

By this time we were milking five of them. That is to say Greg was milking them. He'd spent his childhood summers on his grandfather's farm, and he knew about milking. On the other hand, my mother had advised me long ago never to learn to milk a cow, the idea being that if you did, that would be one more chore you got stuck with. I think she was speaking from experience. The only hitch was that Greg had to go to the market once a week to pick up the produce for his summer business, supplying fruit and vegetables to the surrounding camps and hotels. He left at three a.m. and did not get back until after ten, so he suggested that it would be nice if I did that one milking. He assured me that it was easy and I should have no problem, so I said I'd try. And I did try. I got the first doe into the stanchion and sat down with my pail and did everything the way he'd shown me. It didn't work. I coaxed about one cup of milk from her. She got pretty restless after she'd eaten all her grain, and it was somewhat of a wrestling match after that. The same thing happened with each of the others. I spent about an hour and a half with the five of them. When Greg got home at ten o'clock he looked at his darlings and asked, "Why didn't you milk them?" That was the end of my milking career. Mother was right.

Goats are by nature curious animals, which is probably how they got their reputation for eating garbage, which they don't. They merely nose around in there to see what it used to be, now and then nibbling on a label. If I happened to have clothes on the line when they ambled by, the clothes quite often wound up frayed. Their usual diet was goat chow and the lower leaves of trees, which they would stand on their hind legs to get to. And, of course, the neighbor's roses.

Goat milk tastes just like cow's milk, but it's naturally homogenized, so the cream doesn't separate. It digests well because the fat globules are much finer. Some people have pre-conceived notions about goat milk. Our new neighbor's son was a frequent visitor. He always commented he "shore wouldn't drink that stuff," so I kept a supply in a Borden bottle just for him. He liked it just fine.

As our herd grew, we were soon awash in milk and puddings and cheeses. A local teacher brought her daughter at kidding time to help explain to her the reproduction processes. One spring we had fifteen kids born in rapid succession in the maternity ward in our new basement. I was assigned to do the weaning. We had kids on three-hour schedules and four-hour schedules, and I seemed to be feeding somebody every hour of the day. It was pretty messy. I was usually covered with milk.

Everybody loved those goat kids—right up until they climbed up onto the hoods of their cars to play king of the mountain.

We went to goat shows with various of our prima donnas, and came home with lots of ribbons. Greg liked to say that his goats had udder perfection. By this time our oldest child had grown to young girlhood, with long blonde hair. She no longer climbed into rabbit hutches, but could often be seen herding those goats back from their latest foray. People began to call her Heidi.

One day one of those little goat kids wandered off and we could not find him. We enlisted the aid of our neighbor, Mr. Myers, who was the school custodian. He and Greg searched far into the night, without success. The next day Mr. Myers was noticeably tired at work. When he was asked about it he said, "Oh, I was up most of the night looking for one of the Gregsons' kids that got lost."

"Oh, did you find him?"

"No, he's still out there somewhere."

This set off a shock wave that took a lot of explaining. The kid finally wound up on a lady's porch about two miles away. She had no idea what that little critter was, and started inquiries, and he was soon home. We named him Lucky. The following fall he was among the surplus bucks that we had butchered. He was delicious.

Every hunting season we worried about some hunter shooting one of our prize goats, and it did happen once. Mostly, though, the hunters that come this far from the city have more sense. Nevertheless, every now and then some inebriated soul would show up at the local bar babbling about the whole herd of deer that he'd just seen.

By 1953 it became clear to Greg that we couldn't manage this burgeoning herd any longer. By this time we had two more children, and he had to make a serious living for all of us. We sold the whole herd to a nice lady in Fort Ann, and he bought a tank of tropical fish.

BACKWOODS GOURMET

October, 1948. There I was, at the ripe old age of 22, living in an old army tent beside a brook about a mile out from a little town in the Adirondacks. I was already a veteran of three years of married life, with a two year old daughter. We were building a house up on the hill, and the tent was only temporary. I have found that temporary is a term used a lot in the Adirondacks. It's something of a permanent condition. The weather was really warm in June when we put up that tent, so we located it near the brook and in the shade. The only thing wrong with that was that now it was October, and cold. And the roof was not on that house yet. I couldn't wait to get to the general store with my two-year-old on cold mornings, and thaw out with hot chocolate and real toast.

We were new to the community. "New" can be a long time in the Adirondacks. And we were not very well acquainted yet. Down the road in one direction was a large farm. Chickens, cows, corn and pastures—a very nice farm. Up the road in the other direction lived a large Adirondack family whose matriarch had taken me under her wing. This woman knew everything I needed to learn. She cooked up veritable blizzards of heavenly food on her big woodstove.

When we decided to butcher a large batch of rabbits, she showed me how to can the meat. Rabbit is really quite tasty; a lot like chicken.

We had lots of rabbits, and it was definitely time to thin them out. We butchered twenty or forty of them. It's hard to remember how many. Besides that there were twelve or fourteen goats to look after, not to mention the flock of racing pigeons, the nine puppies that the dog gave birth to under the floor of the tent, and the three kittens that the cat had on a basket of clean laundry. Oh, yes, and the three Cochin bantam chickens we had brought back from the Rutland Fair: Henry, Henrietta I and Henrietta II.

So then the other nice lady who lived across the road decided to ask me to join the Rebeccas. I was thrilled. I had no idea what the Rebeccas were, but I could hardly wait to find out. What I discovered was that they were the counterpart to the Odd Fellows, one of those benevolent organizations that added some welcome social life to the long winter months.

They did turn out to be very nice ladies, and at the first meeting I attended they were planning a covered dish supper. I soon discovered that at a covered dish supper you are expected to bring a "dish to pass." I was inspired. I went home to my tent and consulted *The Joy of Cooking*, that my mother had given me when I was married. I was still learning to cook, and it was an uphill battle on a two-burner gas hotplate located in a little shelter just outside the tent. We did, however, have a little stovetop oven, which doubled nicely as an extra seat when we had company. Our budget did not include any gourmet touches, but fortune was smiling upon me. There was a recipe in there for Chicken Pot Pie. I figured with just a few substitutions I could produce a large bowl of it. Remember, rabbit tastes a lot like chicken. We had lots of rabbit. I got out my large yellow pyrex bowl—the really big one, and a few cans of mushroom soup, and produced a really tasty potpie with a lovely biscuit topping.

Well, that potpie made a big hit. The only thing was, I noticed as the meal progressed that everyone was requesting another helping of that chicken pie. It occurred to me that I was sailing under false colors. I have always prided myself on being truthful. So finally I found it necessary to mention that it was really a rabbit pie.

The effect was startling. Everything seemed to stop, sort of in midair. The lady from the nice farm down the road turned to me, and I noticed that her face was a rather pale green. She looked at me accusingly and said, "I bet you made the crust with goat milk too, didn't you?" Well, of course I did.

It had not occurred to me that rabbit and goat milk were not considered proper food in this conservative stronghold. Chicken was the proper meat. Also, one did not use goat milk. That's what cows were for. I was somewhat chagrined to learn this.

If you ever want to become a legend in your own time,

this is the way to go about it. The good ladies of the Rebeccas stood by me in spite of my many shortcomings. They tried really hard to straighten me out, and now and then had some success. Over time, though, it became apparent that some things are beyond help. One can only remain tolerant, and they did. I still remember fondly the lovely shower they gave me when we had our fifth child. That fifth child is now somewhat over 40 years old. The other day I had lunch with the lady who used to live across the road. She said, "Do you remember when you made that rabbit potpie?" I really enjoy being a legend.

Tent

ice box

hot plate

stuff

to goat pen
rabbit hutches
pigeon house
brook, etc.

oven

to auxiliary
cooking
facilities

MERRY CHRISTMAS

At our house you could always tell when it was Halloween. It smelled like balsam. Balsam is a kind of fir tree, very aromatic, used extensively in the northeast for Christmas trees and wreaths. As soon as I came east to the Adirondacks I was introduced to balsam fir. I thought somebody must be kidding. The only balsa I'd ever heard of was the very soft wood my brothers had used for model airplanes. As usual, I was wrong.

My father-in-law had been in the nursery business on Long Island, and when he had come to the Adirondacks, almost his first thought had been, "Wow! We can make wreaths and sell them 'down on the island'." So when his son, Greg, and I showed up after the war (World War II, of course) practically the first activity we took part in was wreath making. It came right after hunting season. Greg and his father brought huge bundles of balsam from their woods, and we all got together in the barn and made wreaths. It was not a small operation. We wholesaled them by the thousand. We used balsam by the ton.

In 1946 I became somewhat of an authority on Christmas trees. That was the year when Greg and his father were Christmas tree merchants. In October they went to Nova Scotia to cut trees and arrange shipping to Long Island. I found it amazing that Christmas trees were cut in October, and came from Canada, but I didn't dwell upon it. I was preoccupied with feeling sorry for myself, left at home with the baby. They came back in time to go hunting, and then we made thousands of wreaths out of good Adirondack balsam fir. Those wreathes were loaded on the truck and went with them to Long Island, where they sold everything. I was left at home again, with the baby, and no Christmas tree. It was clearly time for me to pull myself together and become self-sufficient. On Christmas Eve I ventured out into the woods and cut a nice shapely tree, brought it in, propped it up, and decorated it. I felt rather accomplished.

On Christmas day, my husband arrived back in town on the bus. I cranked up the Model A—yes, really—and drove in to town to bring him home. As soon as we came in the door, his nose wrinkled and he asked, "What is that awful odor? It smells like a cat."

At that point in our lives, we had no cat.

Finally he noticed my lovely Christmas tree.

Good Lord!" he said. "You've gotten a cat spruce!"

Well. I had never heard of a cat spruce. It looked like a Christmas tree to me. I had sort of wondered what that odd odor was.

We didn't have that tree very long.

Also, Greg never went off to Canada and Long Island

again to be a Christmas tree merchant. It was no fun, it didn't pay very well, and who knew what he'd be coming home to?

Mr. Gregson was a meticulous wreath maker. After only two years of clipping and bunching, I was allowed to tie a wreath. Under his watchful eye, I became an expert. By the time he went on to other things, Greg and I were thoroughly into the wreath making business.

As our family grew, the wreath routine continued, and so every Halloween the whole process began again, usually in our basement, and the whole house would smell of balsam again. Our children were all trained to know they had to look after themselves to a certain degree, and I used to surface every now and then to do a little baking, get a meal, or collapse on the living room couch. When the boys were old enough they were out with their father, bringing in tons and tons of balsam, and some of them got really good at clipping and bunching for me. We had them all convinced that Christmas depended upon them.

We finished up all those wreaths just before Christmas and then we went shopping. By that time, everyone else was done, so there were interesting sales. Greg loved those bargains, and whatever was on sale was what those kids got for Christmas. One Christmas it was guns that shot Ping-Pong balls. There was war raging all over the house, and some of those balls showed up later during the Easter egg hunt.

Every wreath season we indulged ourselves in a housekeeper once a week to keep us somewhat cleaned up. We had a very nice lady come and do the scrubbing. Jenny was a no nonsense person and the whole house shone when she was done. The odor of ammonia actually overtook the balsam for the day. Once she cleaned my oven with sandpaper. Do you suppose that was a comment on my housekeeping? In the afternoon when I drove her home I usually had an assortment of children with me. We stopped at the grocery store, and I cruised the aisles at a rapid clip saying no to all childish requests. Jenny always admonished me for being such a mean mother and bought them each a treat. They loved her.

One year at the end of wreath season we said goodbye to Jenny again and she presented me with a new sponge mop, advising me to use it frequently. That Christmas my mother's present to me was the services of a housekeeper once a week for the whole year. I called Jenny right away to tell her about it. She said, "Humph, If I'd known that was going to happen, I'd have given you a better mop." For a whole year we were nice and clean.

The selection of our own Christmas tree was always a serious business, and it was always a balsam fir, carefully chosen by our former Christmas tree merchant. Except for the year when we lived in a small modern house in the wilds of Sullivan County, at the entrance to a Boy Scout camp. It was one story, with sliding glass doors opening at ground level, and clerestory windows above, up to a twelve-foot peak. I told Greg, "We need a Christmas tree that goes all the way to the top."

He said, "If we have one that big, we'll have to move out. The living room is only twelve feet wide."

But he solved the problem. He found a twelve-foot balsam tree, trimmed all the branches off of one side, and stood it right up against the window. Then he got a twelve-foot white pine tree, trimmed all the branches off one side, and put it up against the window on the outside. Voila! We had an indoor-outdoor tree! We decorated both sides, complete with lights. Passing motorists had a tendency to slam on their brakes. It was fun.

Finally, we moved to an old barn on top of a hill, back in the Adirondacks again. We made it our home and wound up with a seventeen-foot ceiling, and lots of room. Naturally, we had to have a seventeen foot Christmas tree every Christmas. Those trees got so they dominated things. We left them up longer and longer. They were a great challenge to decorate. All sorts of festivities happened around them. The "Taking Down the Tree Party" became a large social event, culminating in a blazing inferno in our oversize fireplace.

These days I go and make wreaths for a florist I know who appreciates the handwork. It keeps me out of trouble for the entire month of November. I go through four or five pair of gloves and about that many tons of balsam and have a wonderful time. I notice that I'm slowing down a bit, though, and this year my work shirt sort of fell apart. Gee, it was only about twenty years old. So I told my employer maybe it's time for me to retire. She bought me a new shirt.

As for my Christmas tree, I usually get a tiny one for the tiny house where I live now. But that's OK, cause I'm not there very much. I'm off seeing what they're using in each of my children's homes. They are all real Christmas tree connoisseurs.

child Labor

WHEELS

We started out married life in 1945 with a '36 Ford coupe that my husband had used during the war to court a local girl in between convoys to Europe. The courtship was in vain. She turned him down. It was nothing personal. It was just that he seemed intent upon living in these Adirondack Mountains, and she couldn't wait to leave.

The '36 Ford had a leaky radiator. We carried a pail with us, and kept an eye out for ponds and streams wherever we went. Very soon we abandoned that car and bought a Model A for fifty dollars from a man in Lake George. That was an interesting car. There was a lever on the steering wheel that regulated the gas mixture, and during the winter months it was necessary to use a crank to persuade it to start. I always tell everybody that I learned to drive on a Model A.

Where I came from, I didn't need to drive. With few exceptions, there were busses for every place I wanted to go. But there weren't any busses on these back roads in the Adirondacks, so I had to learn to drive.

Not that I hadn't taken a crack at it before. The year when I lived with my brother in Texas he tried to teach me to drive his gorgeous red Pontiac convertible. His technique was a bit unusual. He decided one night when we'd gone a few miles out of town for dinner that it was time. He climbed into the passenger seat and said, "OK, now, you drive us home.

I lurched through the gears somehow, but I could not persuade my foot to rest lightly on the gas pedal. I was too nervous. We careened madly homeward. Since I am now writing this, you know that we made it, but my brother became a lot less interested in my driving lessons after that. I remember standing on corners waiting for busses, watching people shift gears as they drove by, wondering how they could manage to do all those things with their hands and feet at the same time and still remain calm.

However, now it was time to learn to drive or be stranded. So I learned. The nice thing about a Model A is that whatever goes wrong can usually be fixed with a little tape or a piece of wire. Also, it couldn't go fast enough to get into much trouble. There was one time, though, when the brakes failed at the same time as the steering went, and I ran over Aunt Florence's petunias.

Our two-year-old daughter usually accompanied me. She would stand in front of the passenger seat and hold onto the dashboard. That way she could see where we were going. It was also the only way she could brace herself for the rattly car and the bumpy road. I had the steering wheel. This was before seat belts, but high speed crashes were not a problem.

When we acquired various animals and started to build a house, we decided to sacrifice the ping-pong table, and Greg used it to make a new back for the car so we could carry supplies. After that, people referred to it as Gregson's Town and Country. He made a roof for it out of tin, which kept coming loose and flapping in the breeze. We were pretty easily recognized going through town. One day the neighbor's son, who was helping with the work, decided to have a little fun. While I was shopping, he tied the gearshift to the brake pedal. Suddenly the car became very hard to manage. I went barreling up the main street of town trying to keep out of the way of things while he howled with laughter. Greg suddenly got a lot of calls from people reporting that his wife was speeding through town. I should mention that the speed limit was a lot less than it is now. Besides, how fast can a Model A go?

After about two years of driving around, it occurred to us that some day someone might want to see my drivers license, so I'd better get one. It didn't look as though the Model A would pass inspection, so we borrowed his father's Hudson pickup truck. That was impressive. It was about three times longer than our little car, and the motor was very quiet. I drove gingerly through Warrensburg and Lake George and parked at the curb in Glens Falls. A grumpy old man climbed in to give me my test.

I have poor hearing. My first mistake, after turning the key, was to ask, "Is the motor running?" I could tell by his expression that it was, so I flapped my hand out the window and started out. In 1948 there were no turn indicators. You had to use hand signals. We got into an argument about whether I had signaled before I left the curb, and I hadn't even gone around the block yet. Then he had me do a K turn in a driveway. I ran that big truck over both curbs. By the time we returned he was so disgusted, he climbed out and disappeared. I told Greg it was no use, and we drove home under our own little black cloud. Three days later my license came in the mail. I guess he never wanted to go through that again.

We had some good times in that little car. We drove it cross country, and up on top of the sawdust pile in our back yard. One evening we were driving down route 9 when a shiny new Buick passed us. Greg became incensed. He said he didn't like the superior attitude of that Buick. We speeded up and passed that car with the throttle wide open and the roof banging indignantly. After that incident our little car was never quite the same. The little motor had just given its all. We put it out to pasture behind the sawdust pile where the daisies could grow right up through the floorboards, and we acquired a green '39 Ford pickup truck.

That truck was big enough to carry loads of rabbit chow and take the goats to shows. It was a good thing we lived on that hill, because usually the way you started it was to head down the hill, working all the gadgets. Most of the time it started by the time you reached the bottom.

After that there was a blue Plymouth sedan, and then there were dozens of station wagons. The bigger our family got, the bigger the car. But that's a whole other story.

44

Gregson's Town and Country

ADIRONDACK ECONOMICS

During World War II I got a really good dose of working for a large company, eight hours a day, six days a week.
And I don't mind telling you it was a drag. I remember
returning home after work wondering whether that was all
there was going to be. I must have unconsciously looked for
the kind of husband who would not want to be a cog in any
big wheel, because that's what I got.

I don't think it ever occurred to him to look for that
kind of a job, and the few times he settled for anything like
that he was desperately miserable. Which was only one of the
many reasons why he was so happy in the Adirondacks. It
takes a certain kind of personality to live there. I could give
you a fast history of Adirondack settlers to prove my point,
but the fact is that the place is inhabited with unconventional
individuals.

During the war, Greg's only experience had been as
Gunners Mate Second Class in charge of a gun crew. That
doesn't translate into anything in particular in civilian life. He
could have gone to college on the GI bill, but that sounded a
lot like conformity. He'd had three and a half years of conformity in the navy and that had been plenty.

So, after hunting season was over, it was time to survey the situation. There was construction going on at a hotel in Schroon Lake, paying one dollar per hour. And then there was a stint on a snowplow. There was plenty of snow. After that there was work at the "mouse factory," a nearby establishment that raised mice for laboratories.

By that time it was summer, and he and his father established a vegetable route supplying hotels and resorts from the market in Menands. It was interesting to notice what was being served at the various establishments. There were always calls for mushrooms when the meat was getting old. We were kept busy in the afternoons delivering half crates of lemons and celery to frantic cooks who had forgotten to order them.

Greg and his father also discovered bargains in war surplus supplies, and they were supplying GI mosquito dope to general stores all over the Adirondacks. We discovered quite by chance that it made a great paint remover. The only time I lost my cool was when I found one of our children pouring a bottle of it over the head of another one, with it running down into his eyes. I panicked and called the doctor, who told me not to worry, just wash it off. I always panicked at the wrong moments.

Everything came to a screeching halt when it was hunting season. All his buddies showed up from Long Island, and feeding them was a challenge. Of course, everything tasted wonderful after a day in the woods, and since I had only recently taken up cooking, their praise was all the impetus I needed. Hunting season rushed by in a flurry of mashed potatoes, trail stew, venison, rolls, pies and cake.

After that we made wreaths by the thousand for the Christmas season, and then there was the logging. I remember at one point being on one end of a crosscut saw wondering whether there wasn't a better way. Very soon chain saws were invented. They were heavy and smelly and prone to breakdown, but when they worked they cut a lot of wood, so he decided to become a chainsaw dealer. I said, "Those things will never catch on." Fortunately, he paid no attention. He set up shop in our basement and soon the air was blue with the revving of motors. I would be entertaining pleasantly inebriated French Canadians while he wrestled with their chain saw problems, or searching desperately through the parts department for parts that never seemed to be there. The chain saw yellow made a nice color for our new front door. Perhaps that's what inspired one son to use a spray can of it to decorate his brother. I was not pleased that he had chosen to do this operation in the middle of our bed on a new blue blanket.

Later on there was the Cedar Pole Company. Greg and his father were shipping forty-foot poles to New York City, and there would be calls in the middle of the night from truckers broken down in Poughkeepsie. There was also the horse, his name was Prince, who had to be fed, housed, and kept in shape to skid the logs. When we acquired a tractor to replace Prince, it sounded like a great idea. Greg took me out into the

49

woods to admire it, but I was greatly disappointed to see that it was not even as big as our car, and cost twice as much. On cold mornings when he had to light a fire under it to get it started, I was thankful to be needed at home.

Observing other rugged individuals coping with North Country reality, it seemed to me that fast footwork was the key to survival. The neighbors with sugar bushes kept hopping twenty-four hours a day in the spring, and had a wondrously sweet aroma about them. The farmer up the hill, who kept us supplied in lovely un-pasteurized milk and large, brown eggs, was busy converting his fields to stands of Christmas trees. His wife had no trouble cooking on her wood-stove, and didn't seem to mind keeping the fruit tree covered with her lace curtains to protect the fruit from the birds.

There were, of course, hermits out there in the woods. They seemed to enjoy their solitude, and were well adapted to the "howling wilderness" theme. Some of them were not above flaunting it at outdoor shows in various cities. However, that lifestyle did not include wives and children. So for Greg, it was too late to be a hermit. The smaller cuts of cedar were in great demand for fences, to discourage forays of deer into orchards and gardens, and this helped pay for our tunafish and noodle casseroles.

One year he was called to jury duty. By that time we had four children and a whole barnyard full of animals, (few of whom were contributing to our well being, by the way) and he asked to be excused. The judge asked him what he did for a living. "Well," he said, "It depends on which season." He began a recital of all his various occupations. When he got to about one dozen, the judge excused him.

Every now and then I used to read about the post war prosperity. I used to sit on the porch steps and wonder when all that prosperity would get to the Adirondacks. It never happened.

ADIRONDACK ENTREPRENEUR

If you've ever driven any distance through the Adirondacks, you've probably noticed a whole lot of FOR SALE signs. We who live here are pretty much used to these and pay very little attention until a sojourner from elsewhere remarks about it. Then I find that before I have a chance to really explain the phenomenon, the recipient has acquired that glazed look and I know it's just too complicated.

Except that it's really pretty simple.

It's this way. Everybody's big dream is to find a way to come to the woods and live the simple life. A whole lot of people will allow themselves the luxury of considering the matter. They will spend their summer vacation in a campground or cottage contemplating the possibilities. They will watch the locals scurrying busily around making money, and then they will sit at the beach, or out in their boat (for which they have paid plenty) fishing, and mulling it over. They might even come early for the fishing, or later for the hunting; or even in the winter with their skis or snowmobiles. It all seems so invigorating and inviting!

After awhile they might encounter an ad in a local paper, listed under "Business Opportunities." This ad will talk about a cozy little mom and pop store in a small Adirondack town, or a motel, or campground—sometimes a whole "Adirondack Attraction." This is a real temptation; a chance to be your own boss.

They might visualize waking up in the morning and breathing all that fresh air. How about eliminating that stop and go traffic. How about eliminating that boss!

Suppose you actually answer that ad.

Before you can say, "Barkeater," you are the new owner of a piece of The Adirondacks. Forget about the hassle with the APA. Never mind that the neighbors look at you suspiciously. They probably think you're financed by the Mafia. You got this fixer-upper for a song, and you're going to set the world on fire!

And it's true. You really are the boss, and, as Harry Truman would say, "the buck stops here," or at least pauses on its way by.

Pretty soon when you wake up in the morning that good fresh air you've been breathing seems to be a little frosty, and is coming in through walls that need insulation. The gorgeous fireplace consumes cords and cords of wood that need to be cut and hauled and split and stacked and stoked. It makes ashes that need to be cleaned out and disposed of. And another thing. You'd better make sure the chimney is cleaned. You don't want a chimney fire.

Also, that pure and delicious water you're drinking probably comes from a well whose pump works all right, except when the power goes off, and it will need replacement whenever there's a summer storm and it gets struck by lightning. And it's true. You're avoiding all that traffic, because there isn't any. Summer is over and all the business you were expecting has evaporated.

Don't worry, you tell yourself. Summer will come again, and you'll get rich. Meanwhile you have long, meaningful conversations with your friendly neighborhood banker, and you carefully plan your strategy. You place ads in an amazing array of publications, each of which claims to have superior coverage of prospective vacationers. The prices are astonishing. Then you pay the taxes and the insurance, and make the mortgage payment. Then you discover that the "fixing up" is costing more than you had figured (it always does). And everything you need is far, far away, and nobody delivers. You're probably going to get involved in that traffic again, only this time it'll be with a truck. Notice how much more room you need?

You will find yourself looking for a job in order to make ends meet—just until summer comes. But there just don't seem to be any jobs. Except maybe grooming ski trails, or subbing as a school bus driver, or snow plowing. They don't seem to pay very well. You get to be an expert at deficit spending. Your responses to overdue bills become extremely imaginative.

Finally it's spring again. The ice breaks up in the lakes. The driveway you had to shovel is now too muddy to navigate, and the day of the black fly is at hand. You are feverishly preparing for the summer season, begging for suppliers to put you on their lists.

Before you are quite ready, it's summer and the tourists appear. Is this when you get to discover the joys of being your own boss? No. This is when you discover that you have a new boss, and it is the customer. You will remain cheerful while people gasp at your outrageous prices. You will commiserate over each errant bug bite. You will apologize for each and every inconvenience. You will remain calm when the plumbing malfunctions and the roof leaks. You will also learn to be polite when the health inspector points out insurmountable difficulties.

By the middle of August you will find yourself thinking how nice it would be if everyone just went home and sent money.

When summer is over, you will finally get around to filling out those tax forms about which you have been receiving nasty letters. You will discover that it wasn't so bad—you only lost a few thousand dollars this season. You will make a note to start early looking for winter work. You kind of wonder when you'll ever actually find time to go fishing or sit on the beach ever again.

Congratulations! You've made it through one whole season of being an Adirondack Entrepreneur. With any luck at all there won't be a FOR SALE sign on your little piece of the Adirondacks for at least another few seasons. It's amazing how complicated the simple life can be.

DOWN THE ROAD APIECE

In 1973 we had that gas shortage. It didn't hit the north country until a few weeks after everybody else; until the storage tanks emptied out. But then it hit with a vengeance. We sat at home and watched on our TV's the people lining up in New Jersey at the gas pumps. There was no way for us to line up at gas pumps. We couldn't get that far. It got really quiet in these parts. People didn't come here any more. They could conceivably get gas to get here, but there was no way to guarantee that they'd be able to get gas to go home again. So everything came to a screeching halt. No tourists. No deliveries. No work. We hunkered down and watched TV. Two or three weeks after the shortage was over, we came to life again.

That's the way it was. While President Carter was admonishing everybody to drive less and walk more, turn off the extra lights and turn down the thermostat, we huddled under extra blankets, stumbled around in the gloom, and weighed the alternatives whenever we ran out of things. The nearest store was not around the corner.

Rural is perhaps a difficult concept for those who have not experienced it. When we say, "down the road apiece," we are talking in miles—not in feet, or even yards. We can't give you the measurement in city blocks, either. I was telling one of my Adirondack grandchildren, one day, how many blocks I had to walk to school in my youth. All grandparents do this, don't they? She asked, "How long is a block?"

I work at a campground during the summer and am often asked where a good restaurant can be found. We have an amazing array of good restaurants in these parts, and they are all—down the road apiece. It's usually easier to tell you how far in terms of road time rather than miles, because although it may be ten miles away, it will probably take fifteen minutes in a car. If it were ten city miles, you'd probable need thirty minutes or more. There is not usually a lot of traffic in the way around here. Also, I usually advise a call for reservations because these restaurants are sometimes not open, or may have disappeared entirely, the economics of the situation being what they are. I am constantly amazed at the quality of our restaurants.

You want to be healthy, too. The nearest doctor is apt to be a long way off. About forty years ago, when we were expecting our sixth child, we somehow got the idea that the more children you have, the quicker they come. So, since we didn't want to curtail our activities, we put a mattress in the back of our station wagon in case of emergency, and carried on as usual. I don't think either one of us knew what we'd do with it, but it was a nice security blanket kind of thing. That was the February when Greg was the district commissioner of scouting, and we were invited to every Blue and Gold

Banquet in the district. We stuffed ourselves with creamed chicken and meatloaf, baked beans, peas, mashed potatoes and cake at numerous communities. On the way home, I invariably acquired false labor pains that kept us cruising in the vicinity of the hospital in Ticonderoga until I decided it was all in vain and we gave up and went home, forty miles away. It made for some very late evenings. One time I decided this was it, and I languished in the hospital for all of Washington's birthday before we realized it was another false alarm. It actually took until March 10 to have that child. We never did use that mattress.

At various times I've had commutes of thirty miles or so. Except for the occasional bad weather, it was usually a pleasant drive; not at all the problem that I understand Long Islanders have with bumper to bumper traffic.

A number of years ago I went to a meeting in Lake George of the Lake George-Lake Champlain Regional Planning Commission. I think that was the title. We listened to proposed plans for the region including "a municipal swimming facility for the people of each county, to be centrally located therein." I found that rather impractical, and pointed out that it might be a one and a half hour drive from some parts of Essex County, for instance, to some "municipal swimming facility," and that anyone so foolish as to take that drive would pass six or eight equally suitable swimming facilities on the way. The fellow with the plan looked at me in some confusion and commented that it ought to work; it was good urban planning.

At one point I became the PTA district director for Essex, Clinton, Franklin and Hamilton counties. We had fewer PTA units than one apartment complex on Long Island. It took three hours driving time to attend a meeting at the other end of the district. I enjoyed seeing parts of the Adirondacks that I would not have otherwise encountered. Every winter when I called a district meeting we cancelled and postponed for weeks before it actually happened. When it did actually happen, those winter roads gave us trips that were fraught with adventure.

So, if you don't have a car or pickup truck, or some other kind of wheels, you really don't want to be in this part of the world. There aren't any busses going by your door. Life in the boonies is a good life, but unless you're a good scrounger or farmer, or even if you are, you are always going to be on the road again. When you talk about going to the big city, it's apt to be Glens Falls that you're talking about. I'm sure there's a lot going on in other parts of the universe, but I reckon I'm as busy as I want to be. And I'm a really good country driver.

INTREPID HUNTER

One of the first things I learned when I married this Adirondacker and came to these hills was that when it's hunting season, hunting is what happens. Nothing takes precedence.

As you may recall, I arrived in these parts on the first day of that auspicious season. It was soon apparent that all other activities ceased at this point. The ritual was that the men of the family went out each morning before breakfast to look for tracks, usually in newly fallen snow. No tracks meant that time would be grudgingly given to less important activities, such as going into town for necessities, bringing in wood for the fireplace, and pails of water for washing.

My new husband was anxious for me to discover the joys of the hunt. Never having experienced temperatures lower than about seventeen degrees, I was already impressed with the necessity of preparation, so I put on all his navy cold weather gear, did a little practice with his 22 rifle, and supposed I was ready.

My first discovery was the odd way that a hunt was organized. There were those who were "put on watch," and others who "drove" the deer past them. My assignment was to run through the woods barking like a dog and banging on trees with a stick. There is no way to describe how silly I felt. Also, as near as I could tell, all this was not having the desired effect on the deer. It was with great relief that I accepted my second task, which was to stand on watch. There I stood— and—stood—and stood. I saw nothing. I heard nothing. I could not believe this was the excitement of hunting. I waited in despair for rescue, while my body slowly turned to stone. Finally I was led away on shaking legs. It took a long time to thaw.

That is the entire extent of my hunting experience. I permanently retreated to the kitchen. It was two years before

On Watch

I ever actually saw a deer, although I have eaten a lot of venison.

Greg was a serious hunter. The season runs from late October to early December. We had venison to eat from the first day until some time afterward. He did his own butchering, because it had to be done right and he didn't trust anyone else. He had learned at an early age that the "wild" taste is in the membranes that he carefully trimmed away. That wild taste is really bad. If the butcher doesn't do his job right, the cook's task of covering up that taste is almost impossible. Probably that's why so many recipes for cooking game have elaborate sauces. I never did learn those, except for stroganoff. Greg seemed to cut almost the entire deer into steaks, with just some scraps left over. I got pretty famous for the stroganoff I made with those scraps. The nice thing about stroganoff is that variants like more people or less mushrooms can always be adjusted for.

This came in handy because Greg had a large number of hunting friends who showed up, especially at meal times, with ravenous appetites. There is nothing like tramping through the woods all day to work up a hunger. They would plow their way through the steak and potatoes, the stroganoff, the cookies, cakes and pies with much appreciative comment. This naturally spurred me on to even greater culinary efforts. On the rare occasion when we ran out of venison, I'd produce "trail stew," which they all claimed was a triumph. Trail stew is what you have when you didn't get your deer, and have to settle for plain beef. My dear husband always assured his friends that he taught me how to cook, but nobody believed him, even when he hovered over me while I did those venison steaks to make sure I got them right: black on the outside, pink in the middle.

In the early stages of our house building, we were heating with a fireplace in one end of the house and a kerosene space heater in the other. No matter how Greg planned, there was never enough firewood, so when hunting season came along he left me with a pile of logs and a chain saw. He was such an optimist. That chain saw knew when it had an amateur to contend with, and as soon as the master left it refused to start. I tried to convey this problem to the intrepid hunter, but he was somewhat distracted. He never did notice the cold anyway. Finally, when I began burning the furniture, I managed to get his attention. It was not that our furniture was anything valuable. It was all donations from various attics. But you had to wonder what all those guys would be sitting on after awhile.

One year we made the mistake of having a child right in the middle of hunting season. I would have said poor planning, but in those days planning was seldom a factor. Charley called from Long Island and said, "I'm coming up to go hunting with you."

Greg said, "Gee, Charlie, I don't know. My wife's

about to have a baby." to which Charlie replied, "Oh, I don't mind."

Sure enough, the day after he arrived I got that last burst of energy. I cleaned the house. I baked rolls and cookies and pie. I made pea soup and trail stew. That night Charlie became the baby sitter while we trundled off to the hospital 25 miles away. The nurses were busy with an accident case. Greg held the ether while I produced our fifth child. I don't recall whether the doctor ever made an appearance. Greg got home in time to go hunting next morning. That was one of our more efficient performances.

Hunting season was a big deal all over the Adirondacks. Various teenage boys would disappear from school and a number of business establishments would become dysfunctional for the duration. Halloween had the misfortune of occurring in the middle of it. There was always a big costume party at the school, and we invariably dressed our children in ambitiously contrived costumes, anticipating both praise and prizes. We'd had real triumphs with such things as a skunk, Tinker Bell, Speedy Alka Seltzer, and a gloriously beaded Plains Indian costume. The kids would all be waiting impatiently for their father to return from hunting and transport our exotic crew to the party. As time wore on, I would get more and more anxious. I've never been very good at waiting. By the time he appeared, with no time to spare, I'd have myself worked into a frenzy, and berate the hunter all the way to the school. Once he appeared with a box of chocolates. That was certainly out of character. I was well into raging, "If you think this will make up for your lateness," before I discovered the chocolates were from Charley.

Hunting season was all over by the beginning of December. Everything was a little anti climactic after that. We always sent the neck of the deer to Mrs. Warner, and she supplied us with marvelous mincemeat for our Thanksgiving and Christmas pies. Greg would put away his bow and rifle for another year, and eventually the venison would be gone.

WHEELS II

In 1953, my little sister, back in Seattle, decided to get married. This was an auspicious occasion. I hadn't been back there since our oldest child was three. Now she was seven, and there was a three year old and a one year old. It was clearly time for another visit.

In view of the fact that we were still struggling along trying to figure out how to make a living in the wilds of the Adirondacks, my long suffering husband was not inclined to agree that this was a good idea. He kept pointing out that we had no money. I kept pointing out that this fact never bothered him when he wanted to go hunting. We each had our little blind spots.

There was no way I was going to miss my little sister's wedding. I began a long and arduous campaign, finally convincing my reluctant husband that otherwise he'd get no peace. After all, it was August. The fishing was not that good, and hunting season was not until October.

This trip happily coincided with our need to buy a car. Fortunately, station wagons were just being introduced. We became one of the first in our area to drive one. With only years and years of payments it would actually be ours.

Meanwhile all we had to do was butcher all the rabbits, except for the few we sold, along with their hutches. And then sell all the goats, along with their pedigrees, to a nice lady in Fort Ann. And then find a new home for the racing pigeons, and the chickens, and arrange for the neighbors to look after the cats and dog.

The early station wagons were built like panel trucks with windows. I guess the main difference was that the back door opened horizontally instead of vertically. There was a lot of room in there; especially head room. We put all the luggage on the bottom. On top of that was a 4 x 8 sheet of plywood. That held a large mattress where we put our sleeping bags and a car bed for the baby. The children traveled happily back there, making little nests for themselves and flopping over to sleep whenever they wanted to.

Finally it was the middle of August. We were down to $200 and scheduled to leave the next morning at 5 a.m., and Greg was full of doubt.

"We can't afford this," he said.

I wept.

We left the next morning at 5 a.m..

The first leg of our trip was through Canada. Canadian gas was expensive, and Greg was determined not to buy any. At 10 p.m. that night we reached the ferry at Sault Ste Marie and the gauge was on empty. We didn't run out of gas, though, until we were in line for the ferry. Nobody could get around us. We had to be pushed on, and then pushed off again on the other side. The only one embarrassed was me. Everybody else seemed to enjoy it.

Greg was the kind of driver who rarely stopped for anything. We camped in cornfields and lovers lanes, washed diapers in irrigation ditches, swam at the Fort Peck Dam on the Missouri River, spent an afternoon at Glacier National Park, and arrived at Seattle in four days, exhausted and happy. It was a lovely wedding.

The trip back was another whirlwind affair. We discovered that we could make lots of mileage just before dawn while the children slept, and could even stop for coffee and toast while they slumbered on. One day inland from either coast we could get eggs with the coffee and toast for the same price, and near the Mississippi we could get "the works;" toast, eggs, hash browns, and a happy smile too!

Our return to the Adirondacks found us not much more destitute than if we hadn't gone. The seven year old had discovered numerous west coast cousins and the three year old had learned to say pain packs (train tracks).

As the years went by, we progressed through ever larger station wagons, and our family grew right along with them. One of those station wagons had a rear seat that faced backward, leaving a little space between that and the second seat just large enough for a car bed for the current infant. We called it the poop deck.

We made three or four more trips that way and acquired a tent trailer in due course for the extra bodies. Our children were all brainwashed to know that the best souvenir from anywhere was a rock. So we have agates from the Olympic Peninsula, rose quartz from South Dakota, water tumbled glass from the Great Lakes, and pretty rocks, driftwood and shells from everywhere.

At some point during my children's' school careers the teacher asked who had been outside of New York State. When my offspring mentioned where he'd been, never mind that he'd been only an infant at the time, the reaction of his classmates was, "Yeah, sure you were."

CHILDREN ARE DURABLE

My husband was always good in emergencies. That turned out to have been a real advantage, because our usual condition was a state of emergency. He was a master at applying butterfly bandages to all wounds that lesser individuals might have taken to the doctor for stitches. My children have various scars as souvenirs of his handiwork.

Actually, in our family, one would need to be really hurting before any particular notice would be taken. There was always too much going on. If you fell in the lake, for instance, before you had quite learned to swim, one parent or the other would usually pluck you out by your overall straps. Most cuts, bruises and abrasions got better by themselves. Children are very durable.

Our youngest son was unusually accident prone. He actually required stitches so often that his tetanus shot was always current. He fell out the back window of the station wagon. He put his hand through the French door. He ran full tilt into the pillar of the garage. He invented a catapult that successfully threw a large rock into his forehead. We usually slapped him onto the doctor's examining table, got him sewed up again, and made off with him. The only time he wept and wailed was when we encountered an over-solicitous nurse. Apparently he felt he shouldn't disappoint her. One child fell into the pond in back of our house and his brother came in to tell us about it. "He made the prettiest bubbles!" he said. I became a little concerned, and asked, "Well, where is he now?"

"Oh, he's coming."

Sure enough, in came the three-year-old, dripping wet. He assured me that he had fallen off the dam. I asked, "How did you get out?"

He said, "Oh, I walked out."

It reminded me of his father.

One cold spring day when the ice was breaking up, another young son found himself adrift on a little island of ice in another small pond down our hill. While his brother went for help, he saved himself by jumping in and walking out. He came up the hill, soggy and frozen blue. His father put him in the tub and scrubbed him vigorously, but he stayed blue. Greg was beginning to panic, rubbing furiously, when we realized that the boy's new blue jeans had faded all over him.

After a few years I thought it might be a good idea to take a first aid course. When the class got to the part about poisons, and I told them about all the various things my children had already ingested, they almost gave up on me. There was the one toddler who had climbed up into the bathroom sink, opened the medicine cabinet and had a few swigs of

Bactine. I reckon for awhile he was a really clean kid, both inside and out.

In the Adirondacks you don't really need to worry too much when your children wander off. They're only out in the woods. They always come back. Before I learned that, I gave the neighbors some bad times out helping me beat the bushes, and they never let me forget that.

One afternoon the six-year-old and the four-year-old took the two-year-old out into the woods and left him there. They figured he was one too many. They were a little disappointed when I made them show me where, and brought him back. When he got a little older they included him in the fun. All three decided to leave home one afternoon instead of having their naps, and I went after them. They laughed. They went in three different directions. It took me all afternoon to round them up. After that, whenever anybody threatened to leave home, I just offered to help with the packing.

I used to have nightmares about the missing shoe. Every school day there would be at least one shoe missing when the school bus arrived. One Sunday I was working hard at getting five children presentable for Sunday School. It was my turn to take them while Greg stayed home with the baby. It was the usual lost shoe routine and I was more than usually impatient. I put the beans on to cook and did my ultimatum thing, and went out to wait in the car. It was five miles to church, and I hate being late. Finally they came straggling out while I raced the motor. They climbed in the back, and I pulled smartly out of there.

"Mommy!" four voices screamed. "Blair's not in yet!" Sure enough, the youngest one had been only halfway into the car. When I backed out, the door had knocked him down, and I had backed right over him. There he lay in a little mud puddle in the gravel driveway. I jumped out and ran to him. He looked up at me and said, wonderingly, "Mommy, you ran over me."

I was terrified. I said, "Don't move." and went running into the house to get Greg. When we ran back, there was a little circle of children looking down at the fallen one. Greg knelt down and felt all over the little three-year-old body. Everything seemed to be in order. Nothing was broken. All arms and legs were functional. We picked him up and laid him in the car. We bundled up the baby and took everybody with us and drove into town to the doctor's office. The doctor laid him carefully on his table and examined him. "Are you sure you ran over him?" he asked. He pulled off his pants to get a closer look and there across his hips were the tire tracks. We could not find any other evidence. Our theory was that he had fallen into a slight depression in the driveway, and I had driven across him so quickly that no harm was done.

The doctor advised us we should take him to a hospital for overnight observation, in case of internal injuries. The hospital was a forty-mile drive. As usual, his brother got carsick. Blair had a lovely overnight stay at the hospital. The nurse was a former baby sitter of ours.

The beans, however, got burned.

After that, for months, whenever I took Blair anywhere, he always admonished me, "Now don't run over me, Mommy."

But it's like I said. Children are durable. Forty years later I was invited, along with one of my other sons, to dinner with friends of his. It was a lovely occasion and I was enjoying being a lady. Then, during a lull in the conversation, this son of mine interjected, "Say, Maw, tell them about the time you ran over Blair."

My past keeps haunting me.

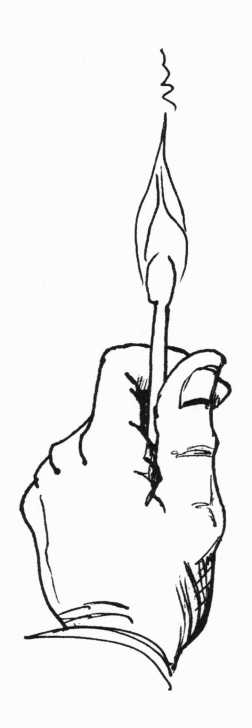

PYROMANIA

My oldest daughter is very timid about fire. Of course, she has always been rather compulsive about doing everything properly. She's the one who could not learn to play our little organ because she didn't want to strike a note unless it was the right one, but she couldn't be sure it was unless she played it. Think of the frustration! She is also very timid about fire. It might be because fire can be rather unpredictable, but I think it's because her brothers were such pyromaniacs.

There was, for instance, the four year old who went outside every afternoon about two o'clock and started a grass fire while I was putting his brother to bed for his afternoon nap. There I would be in my ungainly pregnant condition out there beating the grass with a broom. He could count on my undivided attention every afternoon at two. Very soon he was introduced to other more acceptable methods for gaining my attention, and eventually kindergarten intervened, to the relief of all of us.

There was also the ten year old who was interested in chemistry. He wanted to see what would happen to a particular mixture he'd put together if he heated it, overlooking the fact that he was using a plastic pitcher, which burned furiously. It was not a good thing to have happen in our basement.

Of course, the eight year old had no idea that he would be starting a forest fire. He just wanted a little picnic cookout on the ridge under the big pines, on ground about four inches deep with dry pine needles. We let the forest ranger explain it to him after they had put it out.

On one occasion when we had just moved into a new community, I was introduced to the local lumber yard owner the hard way. He came knocking at my door to inform me that two of my boys were having a campfire in his lumber yard. It was not the best way to become acquainted.

Later on, they built a fort out of hay bales on the edge of a neighboring farmer's field, and then decided to have a nice warm fire. The resulting conflagration was spectacular and destroyed their fort.

The younger ones did not seem to learn from the experiences of the older ones. At one point we were living at a large Boy Scout camp. One of mine, and a neighbor's boy received permission to spend the night at a lean-to down by the lake. They spent the day getting ready. While they were about it, they decided it would be nice to have a kerosene lamp, so they went up to the storehouse and got one, along with a supply of kerosene, which they brought back to the lean-to. After filling it, slopping a little on the plank floor, they decided to test it.

A scoutmaster, who had been out on the lake in a

canoe, later described it to me. "I saw this blaze," he said, "so I paddled across to see what it was. There were these two boys running back and forth to the fire carrying plastic cups of water from the lake."

Fortunately, the camp had a fire truck handy, but the lean-to burned to the ground, with all the boys' camping gear. The story we got from the boys was somewhat different than the other version, but they didn't go camping that night, or for some time afterward.

Since then, all our boys have become experts at building, using and putting out fires. So far, I haven't heard of any grandchildren having the same kind of adventures their fathers did. Do you suppose they've imparted to them some of their hard-earned wisdom? Or is it maybe that they'd rather not talk about it?

The Happy Man

VROOM, VROOM

Being of the female persuasion, I'm not sure what
comes first in the hearts of men; whether it's hunting, fishing,
contact sports, war maneuvers, speed or rearranging the landscape. I have had occasion, however, to notice the happy preoccupation of the male of the species with heavy machinery.

It must be the feeling of power.

I can still recall the delighted anticipation that my husband evidenced when replacing the workhorse with the bulldozer, back when he was in the logging business. He showed
it to me with great pride, and hardly noticed my lack of enthusiasm. It looked so small to me. And the payments looked so
large. He took good care of his machine and became quite an
artist with it, skidding logs down what looked to me like sheer
cliffs, using the untrimmed branches on the logs as brakes.

At one time we lived at a place called Pack Forest, and
there was a nice pond behind our house, which froze every
winter and made a nice skating rink. During the Christmas
holidays one year, there was about two feet of snow out there.
His parents came for dinner, and Greg and the kids decided to
go skating while his mother and I did the cooking. That was a
lot of snow cover, so he decided to get the little bulldozer and

clear it off. Ten year old Eric was standing on the dock watching when everything began to shake.

"Daddy, Daddy," he yelled, "The ice is cracking!"

Greg paid no attention. He was happily scraping away when suddenly everything sank. The bulldozer was hung up on a ledge about ten feet down. Greg was soaked. He came sogging sheepishly into the kitchen where his mother and I were fixing dinner.

His mother said, "Don't let your father see you like that."

No sympathy there.

Then he had to go get a cable and swim back down and hook it under everything to keep it from slipping further down. He needed lots of thawing after that. Next day his crew of men from the saw mill got out the big machine called the bridge builder, probably left over from WWII, and pulled it out. After they dried it out and changed the oil, the little bulldozer worked as good as new. They never let him forget that episode.

Years later, when he built our campground, he had another little bulldozer, and he laid out roads with it, between the trees. Then he carved out campsites. One day he'd been up the hill working away at some stubborn rocks. He came down to the house at noontime and said, "How would you like a pond?"

I said, "We don't need a pond. We need campsites."

So he went back up and carved out a nice little pond. It was his pride and joy. The campers loved it, too. He used that bulldozer and an old dump truck to build the whole place, happily rearranging his landscape. He dug a place for a pool, laid out a septic system and a leach field and excavated for another restroom building. In between, he pulled people out of ditches and plowed the driveway in the winter. He was looking forward to a new dump truck and a front-end loader when he had his last heart attack and died.

There was so much unfinished business. It was only a few weeks after the funeral when I looked out the window and watched his son on that bulldozer, heading out to fix a patch of roadway. He sat that seat in the same relaxed manner that his father had. He looked comfortable.

The shed where we kept the bulldozer parked was just across the way from the office where we checked in the campers. Without fail, all male members of the species would look out there and go, "vroom, vroom." whenever they saw it. Whether they were three or ninety-three years old, they all fairly itched to get on it and gooo. Little girls never seemed to go "vroom, vroom" like that.

Women who have no mechanical ability should not own bulldozers. That fact was pointed out to me on numerous occasions, particularly when it needed repairs. At one point I traded the deer rifle for a new set of treads. I have no idea who got the better of that deal.

Then I rented it to a local excavator who had done

some work for us. That was a mistake. I should have remembered the time he was cleaning out our septic system and the whole back end of his tank truck fell into the hole. He had to go get a log skidder to pull it out.

It seemed to me that this fellow kept my machine quite awhile. Every now and then he would report that he was cleaning and lubricating it and painting it. He seemed eager to keep me informed. One day I got a call from the dealership where my bulldozer was waiting for about $2300 worth of repairs. I had to take that fellow to small claims court and was able to collect $1000. After that I sold it to a neighbor who not only understood machinery, but also kept everything in good repair. Twenty years later, I drove past his place and there he was, tooling along on that old bulldozer, looking good.

Vroom, vroom.

CLIMB EVERY MOUNTAIN

I have always talked a good line about my prowess in the great outdoors, and abilities in the wilderness. And that's just what it has always been: a line. I reckon that's how I got into all this trouble in the first place.

My husband was a wilderness person. He had a lot of professions, but he was mainly a forester. It came naturally to him. He seemed to have been born knowing all about trees, animals, birds, fish. He met me during a period of instability while he was 3,000 miles from his home in the Adirondack woods, and when I gave him this woodsy line of mine he was just naturally interested. My bluff was called.

Eventually I found myself faced with the prospect of climbing some of these Adirondack hills. Greg had seen the Cascade Mountains in Washington State where he'd found me, and we both knew that the Adirondacks were nowhere near that high, so he naturally assumed that I'd have no problem.

Did you know that the best blueberries grow among the rocks up on top of these hills? He may have noticed how I huffed and puffed to climb up there with him, maybe 1500 or 2000 feet, but he never mentioned it. I suppose he was probably accustomed to people lagging behind him on hikes, anyway - way behind.

Eventually, Greg became the Explorer Advisor, and I became the Senior Girl Scout Leader, both at the same time. So when we both were looking to put a little high adventure into our programs, a joint trip up Mount Marcy seemed like a good idea. Mount Marcy is New York State's highest mountain at 5344 feet.

We planned our trip for just after Labor Day, and it was to be a three-day affair, with two nights in a lean-to. My girls were enthusiastic about the idea, and we did a lot of preliminary hiking to get in shape. We even camped out a few nights in our woodlot.

Finally Labor Day was over, and we headed for Newcomb in a pickup truck and a station wagon. Five Explorers, five Senior Girl Scouts, and two intrepid leaders. We drove to the trailhead at Tahawus and hiked in to the first lean-to, which was fortunately unoccupied. I say fortunately because I was pooped. We had walked seven miles, and that was my quota for the day. Also, the lean-to was fortunately large. After we had our supper, we laid ourselves out like cordwood; five girls, me, Greg, and five boys. It worked very well. The Marcy trail was popular, even back in 1957. We had thought the traffic would be thinned out in September, but there were people walking past our lean-to during the night, with lanterns. I have no idea where they went.

The next day it rained. The well trod trail became a busy stream, with muddy islands. One of the boys decided he

86

had a bad cold, and would wait at camp while the rest of us went up to the top and back. We said fine, then he could keep the fire going and cook our soup.

There had been a lot of joking around about the soda fountain on top of Mount Marcy, but today there was no joking. It was much too wet and cold and gloomy for that, and the wind was blowing. The last hundred feet I was pretty sure the wind was going to blow me right off the mountain and I couldn't get any traction, but I was not allowed to quit. They all got behind me and pushed.

There is no magnificent view from the top of Mount Marcy when it's raining. Instead you get the feeling that you're isolated in space somewhere, surrounded by a grey, impenetrable mist. We were eleven cold, miserable ghosts, hunched over and peering out from under dripping hoods. I waited grimly for permission to go back down. When it finally came, I discovered that going down was almost harder than going up. If you didn't dig your heels into the mud, you risked a slippery ride culminating in a muddy seat. If one of my girls hadn't brought extra socks, I'd probably still be up there stuck in the mud. And of course my knees were beginning to creak. It was good to have that hot soup waiting.

Next morning the sun shone again. If you have never watched an otherwise intelligent boy patiently pouring water from his canteen over his spoon to wash it, you've never really camped with kids. We pointed out various alternatives to this technique, but he was not open to suggestion. By the time we had walked the seven miles back to the trailhead, he was drinking enthusiastically from the brook beside the trail. My knees were shaking rather violently by then. They took about a week to recover.

We've been up and down a few other mountains since then. The views have been great. I have learned not to scoff at the relatively low altitudes, since I've discovered that it's the distance up that you climb that counts. It all depends upon where you start from. It's rather amazing how long it took me to learn that.

Years later, I was presiding over the snack bar at our campground while a camper was regaling me with tales of his many adventures worldwide. He'd been to Kilimanjaro and the Alps. He'd seen the Himalayas and the Andes. He remarked that the Adirondacks were pretty tame. Then he went up our trail and got lost.

Mt. Marcy

IT'S THE BERRIES

I don't like fish. Maybe it's the smell, or maybe the bones. I dunno. So then I married a fellow who really enjoyed fishing. He loved to spend hours out in a boat or wading through a brook looking for those slimey little critters and bringing them home to eat. I never quite understood what the attraction was, but he relished those fish.

On the other hand, I'm very fond of berries. There is something exceedingly satisfactory about going out into the woods in that gorgeous summer weather and bringing back something good to eat. Sounds a little like a fisherman talking, doesn't it?

I'm a good berry picker. I'm fast. Also, I don't eat as I pick, because I prefer them cooked. I figure those fishermen and I have a lot in common. We both probably do a lot of deep thinking out there. I recall one afternoon picking my way through a thicket of high bush blueberries while solving all the problems between the Israelis and the Palestinians. Too bad they never asked me.

The berry season in these parts starts out timidly with little tiny wild strawberries that always make you wonder whether it's worth it all—right up until you taste again one of those tasteless monsters from the supermarket. Then there's a pause while you wait for the blueberries to ripen. In between you may find some tender, dewey raspberries. You need to carry them gently or they will turn to mush before you get home. Also keep a sharp lookout for chokecherries. You certainly don't want to eat them. They're much too sour. But they make lovely jelly, cooked with lots of sugar, and if they don't jell, they make really nice syrup for your pancakes when the maple syrup runs out.

Blueberries are the greatest joy to pick, because the bushes have no pricklers. They are sometimes hard to get to, though. The low bush blueberries of the Adirondacks like the rocky places, usually on the tops of these hills. When you finally get up there you can sit on the sun-warmed bedrock and scoop those little blue gems into your pail. And going home afterward is all downhill. I have become quite famous for my blueberry buckle, a juicy coffee cake, stuffed with blueberries and with a crumbly topping.

After that there are the blackberries. I am also well known for my blackberry pie. Those berries like to grow where there has recently been a logging operation. They taste exactly like summer, and you can never get too many. There is a certain air of urgency, though, after awhile, because they're the last real berries of the summer. Pretty soon you'll start to notice the flickers flying by. Those are the big birds with white rumps. When they fly away, they seem to sort of flicker. And flying away is the only way you usually see

90

them. Their presence always means autumn. Then the blackberries will be getting overripe and scarcer, and the bears will
be giving you competition for them, and it will be time to do a
study of the apple trees. My mother-in-law used to munch her
way through the local wild apple trees, locating the best flavor. Then she'd pickle some, and make applesauce, and can a
lot of juice for jelly. That way, next year when the chokecherries won't jell, all you have to do is add some of that apple
juice! I'm not anywhere near as talented a taster as she was,
but I do what I can, and if the applesauce doesn't turn out tasty
I use it for cake.

The last little goodie of the Adirondack wilderness
comes along just after the first frost, and it's the cranberry. It
can be elusive, but we've had some success. You need to
scout around through the bogs for these. One year we found a
really good patch and came home with about two bushels of
cranberries, not quite ripe. We kept them in our basement and
used them as they ripened. We had cranberry juice, jelly, rel-
ish, bread. That was the year (about 1960) when the commercial cranberries from New Jersey bogs were found to be con-
taminated with a spray that caused cancer. We had some
friends over for Thanksgiving dinner that year, and had home-
made cranberry sauce which they politely declined to eat
because of that cancer scare. (We noticed, however, that they
both smoked a lot.)

I should probably mention the grapes, because they do
make really good juice and jelly, but I've noticed that by the

time the grapes are ready I'm about done in. I think we never got too involved with them, because hunting season was close upon us. All that winter preparation had to be done beforehand or we'd be dreadfully unprepared. So we mostly left the grapes to the birds and other wild life. We had already stolen enough from them.

A successful berry season always made it much easier to put up with the fishing and hunting and all the other activities that distracted my otherwise attentive husband. I imagine those distractions made it possible for him to put up with mine. Of course there was the time that he went fishing one time too many and I blew our entire wad—all seven dollars of it—and bought a gallon of paint and painted the ceiling. But that's another story.

BLUE BERRIES!

GINSENG

My husband's grandfather was a wandering farmer. It didn't do any good for his grandmother to try to hide those agricultural magazines, with their ads for herdsmen in other places. He always found them. The story was that he would hire out as herdsman at a nice farm, and stay until he'd harvested all the ginseng in those parts. And then he'd move on. He seems to have farmed all over New York State, and even a little into Connecticut.

There were other things he was famous for in his day. I was told that he invented the curve ball when he was pitching for the Cuyler Hill Boys. He perfected it by curving it around fence posts. That team, they told me, was famous for beating the team that Ty Cobb played for. They called him Big Myron Emory, because he was short.

Anyway, he dug a lot of ginseng in his day, and he taught his son-in-law and his grandson how to find it, too. Apparently, most ginseng harvesters were also trappers. The thing to do was to dry it (the roots, that is) and sell it to the same fellow who bought your pelts. That agent would in turn sell it to a Chinese merchant who would either peddle it in some Chinatown or send it to China. The Chinese, I was told, considered it to be an important aphrodisiac. I remember that part particularly well, because I had to look it up in the dictionary. Everything is so educational. Also, the more gnarled and misshapen the root was, the more power it was supposed to have. I never did find out how they used it - whether it was ground up and used for tea, or sprinkled on things, or maybe they simply gnawed on it. Seems as though, if the shape mattered, maybe it was worn on a string around people's necks. Nobody ever said. When fresh, the ginseng root looks a lot like horseradish, which I know is really potent, ground up with a little vinegar. But this stuff wasn't potent, and after it was dried it sure looked unimpressive.

In 1973, the last time I was ever involved in the sale of some ginseng, it was worth twenty dollars a pound. A few years later I was strolling around the Soho in New York City, and happened into Chinatown. There in a store window was a container of ginseng roots. It was selling for ten dollars an ounce. I asked the proprietor, "Is that stuff any good?"

He smiled knowingly and said, "If you believe—"

Well, I really don't know. The world of medicine keeps changing. Acupuncture, exotic herbs and techniques keep cropping up. The thing that really amazes me is how the price of ginseng has soared since it got "discovered" by the western world. four hundred dollars a pound wholesale sounds rather tantalizing to me, and I've heard it's still going up.

My husband tried to show me what ginseng looks like in the wild, but I was not a good student. I invariably got it confused with something called false ginseng. There was lots of that. Some of our sons, though, got it straight, and one of them has taught his sons. He'd probably teach me, too, if I should ask, but I'm not asking. Not when the DEC is busy tracking down ginseng bandits. I've got enough troubles.

Flora

PADDLE YOUR OWN CANOE

When the ice finally leaves the lakes in these parts, along about the end of April, one of the first things you're going to want to do is get out there on one of these lakes in a boat. The view of the world from the surface of the water is entirely different from what you see by land. The wildlife critters are a whole lot less timid out there, too. It's their more natural habitat.

If you want to get into the wildness of it, though, you don't want to have any kind of a motored boat. All critters will disappear at the first putt of a motor. If you're really in a hurry, there isn't any waterway as fast as a good road, so you shouldn't be out there on the water anyway.

All right. Now that we've got you into a small self-propelled boat, you're on your own. And so am I. My preference is a canoe. I have never had occasion to study sailing. Aerodynamics is a fascinating study, but not my thing. I'm never quite sure what the various maneuvers are good for. Coming about, and beating into the wind, and all that sort of thing are apt to confuse me, and my reflexes are such that as soon as I've figured out what to do it's going to be too late. Also, it seems to me that any body of water that's big enough for a sailboat is also fair game for those motor boats I already warned you about. There goes your peace and quiet.

There is also this beautiful sculpture called the Adirondack guide boat, and it is indeed lovely to look at. There are just three problems with it. (1) I cannot afford one. (2) To make it go, you have to face backward—aft, that is. And (3) I cannot afford one. A rowboat is more affordable, but you also have to row it facing backward, and you don't get to see much that way.

So that's why a canoe is my favorite water craft. Not only do you get to see where you're going, but also you can go it alone if you want to. I really should have mentioned kayaks, but I haven't had much experience with them. I remember watching my brother trying to step into one from a dock. He somehow got caught with one foot on each, and the gap between growing ever wider. He made an impressive splash. I'm pretty sure the audience enjoyed it more than he did. Also I notice that you need to fold yourself up rather abruptly in there, and I'm not at all sure I could still do that. They're fun to watch, though. It's as if the human has become the boat, or vice-versa.

I've seen some really nifty places via canoe, and the maneuvering seems like a natural thing. I particularly like meandering along a peaceful river watching what goes on near the shoreline, feeling like either Lewis or Clark. There might be a beaver who will slap his tail at you, or maybe an otter sliding down a bank. If you find the right lake, you might encounter a loon, or a great blue heron.

Two or three warnings, though. Never let your kids go boating on a windy day—especially if you have anything else planned. They're apt to call you from ten miles away looking for a ride home. Also, don't take the baby canoeing. You can't paddle and keep the kid under control at the same time. Take my word for it. The whole trip is not worth it. Wait till he/she is old enough to paddle his/her own canoe, and can swim. I have avoided many drownings this way. Although kids are durable, there's no sense tempting fate.

Once when we lived at a Boy Scout camp I did a lot of happy canoeing before the scouts arrived. After the camping sessions started it was necessary to pass the test for canoeists, which included the ability to pick up the canoe and carry it to the rack. The canoe was heavier than most of my children at the time. I had to wait till the end of the season. Now there are very light weight canoes available, lighter than quite a few sizes of child. For those I also have advice. If you encounter one without a seat, equip yourself with a cushion. Trust me. You'll need it, both for comfort, and to keep you out of puddles. If there might be rain, don't assume just any rain jacket will do. Make sure you have one with elastic at the wrists. It is most disconcerting to try paddling with a double bladed paddle, with the rain draining down into your armpits with every stroke.

Recently I took my sister and her husband from Alaska on a rafting trip from Indian Lake to North River on the

Hudson. Made the reservations and was most proud of myself to be showing these westerners that New York is not completely paved. Figured we were all prepared. The rafting people shot me down. They insisted on the necessity of their new improved underwear (it was a really cool April) and if my brother-in-law hadn't been equipped with his credit card, we'd have been rejects. That's how I discovered this revolutionary underwear that has seen me through many times since. We emerged from the river many hours later completely soaked, even in our wet suits, and not at all cold. Keep that in mind.

So now that you're all primed and ready, properly dressed, pre-warned about each and every eventuality, go find yourself a buddy and a nice little canoe and become a voyageur. If you have chosen the right partner you won't even need to steer. Just dip your paddle in now and then. But if you're solo, don't be deterred. Just paddle your own canoe.

ADIRONDACK AUTUMN

There is an activity that goes on in the northeast every fall, which some misguided publicist has titled "leaf peeping." That term makes me cringe. It's so cutesy. One can just imagine the plight of the refugee from the city driving aimlessly through the gorgeous autumn colors, gazing at it all surreptitiously through his fingers.

I am embarrased to have to drive anywhere at that time of year for fear that I will be mistaken for a "leaf peeping" tourist.

There are only two things that will squelch my enjoyment of the fall season. That disgusting term is one. Number two is the fact that it is so soon over.

It's a season that starts out with a hurried harvest of blackberries and apples, grapes and squash. The weather is perfect for both hiking and baking. How does one choose? The summer fun people have gone home to their various duties. Only the very wise among them will realize that the best is yet to come. They will be back on weekends. Meanwhile, energy levels are high, and days have purposeful structure again.

One nice thing about autumn is the fact that

Vermonters are such great merchandisers. They have convinced a large segment of the public that the only legitimate place to see Fall Foliage is in Vermont. That way, we Adirondackers can enjoy our own magnificent display without having to cope with the vast number of "leaf peepers" who have unwittingly been lured to Vermont. Let them wallow in all that traffic. Our gorgeous colors have the added contrast of the dark green spruces, pines and firs, and we have lots of reflective ponds for emphasis.

As I said, it is all too soon over. Every glorious day has the underlying threat of winter. You know you should be battening down the hatches, putting up storm windows, covering the wood pile, digging out the snow shovel, cleaning the chimney, repairing the roof. Instead you are hiking, boating, and enjoying life, just like that grasshopper.

Before you even realize what is happening, the blue and gold days of October are gone. The bare branches of the deciduous trees, which were only yesterday sporting all that brilliant color, are now darkly dripping with a cold rain. The hunters are out chasing the elusive deer again, and you are mostly confined to quarters.

You are not compelled to listen any more to "leaf peeping" bulletins. Unless you are a hunter, November is really a nothing kind of month. You might as well go bake some bread and get a start on the Gingerbread Men, because winter is not really going to hit until Christmas is done.

Leaf
peeping

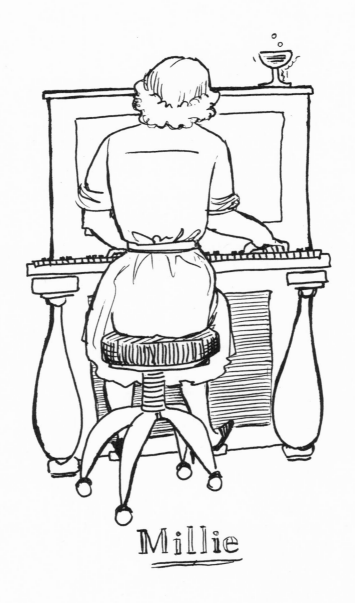

Millie

THE DANCE IS THE THING

You may think that Adirondackers don't dance. You may think they just hunt, fish, cut trees, drink and drive around in their pickup trucks. You'd be wrong. There is a tradition of dancing and music in these parts that goes way back. Before there were many people here at all, there were "kitchen dances" that I understand went on until the wee, small hours of the morning. There seem to be a lot of fiddlers in these hills. I think it's something that runs in families.

By the time I arrived on the scene, in the middle 40s, there were big square dances going on at a large dance hall near Pottersville called The Glendale. I have never discovered how it got that name. Being from the west coast, I naturally assumed they swiped it from that city in California. It was probably the other way around, but that never occurred to me. I'm just as provincial as everybody else is.

I had never done any square dancing, unless you count the Virginia Reels we all did in gym class. Even my jitterbug style was a little hesitant. I had spent most of my USO time during WW II playing ping-pong. I was good at ping-pong, even in high heels and a tight skirt. Greg, however, was really enthusiastic about this square dancing and said I'd enjoy it.

So we went to The Glendale.

A "square" consists of four couples, and the directions were usually quite intricate. It did not help that our first square included his former girl friend who was gorgeous. I had no time to ponder upon that fact, however, because we were soon involved in complicated maneuvers that included a lot of swinging of one's partner, and it was necessary to concentrate upon staying upright. Fortunately, every time things started to blur, some fellow would snatch me from disaster and we would be promenading. Somehow or other, I was back with my own partner when it was all over.

And he was right! I did enjoy it. We did a lot more square dancing after that. I never did attain the nonchalant poker face of the local girls who'd been square dancing since they were born, but I did develop a pretty good shuffle after a bit, so that I would not be mistaken for one of those awkward tourists. I could do-si-do along with the best of them, duck for the oyster, and dive for the clam! It was impossible, though, for either one of us to square dance without big happy grins.

Most of the time, the caller was Art Ingraham. His wife, Millie, played the piano. She always had a glass of creme de minthe handy while she played. I think she was a paperhanger on the side. Gene Specht was the drummer, and Guy LaPell played the fiddle. They all played wonderful, foot tapping music. There was no way your foot would not be tapping. After a few years, Art lost his teeth, and his calling became a little hard to understand, but it didn't matter because everybody knew all the calls by then.

Eastern square dancing, when done properly is pretty smooth, and when a man swings his partner it's usually done with finesse. This is a good thing, because some of these Adirondack women, especially those who work in the woods along with their men, were a pretty good size. When they walked through a door, they filled it. Now and then one of these formidable women would get a partner who wanted to show off his ability to swing her off her feet. At this point, it was not unusual to see her plant both feet firmly on the floor and send that poor unfortunate fellow right into the nearest wall—and sometimes through it.

Somewhere around the mid fifties square dancing went out of style, and Glendale became a skating rink before it petered out entirely, but we enjoyed it while it lasted. Greg's "round" dancing was largely uninspired, so we took up other forms of recreation for a long time. Finally in the late 60s a new thing came along. It was called "Western Style Square Dancing," and for quite awhile it was all the rage in these parts. It involved bouffant skirts for the women and cowboy regalia for the men, and the dances were much more intricate. Greg was back into his old form, and whenever the calls got too complicated, he'd just swing the nearest female and go on from there. It was amazing how well that worked. There is nothing like an evening of brisk square dancing to raise your internal temperature and quicken your metabolism and send you out of the school gym into the sub zero night without any shivering atall.

After Greg died, my dancing days were over. There was a South American gentleman for awhile whose ballroom style was really exceptional, but he went back to Chile. I reckon I'm relegated to the sidelines, but I still enjoy that foot tapping music. You'll see me at those folk music festivals. The beat goes on!

SCROUNGE

When you have lived for awhile in these Adirondack hills, you learn to scrounge. Awhile can be defined in many different ways, depending upon how hungry you've gotten, how disillusioned, how cold; things like that. Definitely more than one season, though. The Adirondack seasons have a way of surprising people. They rarely turn out to be what the newcomer had anticipated.

Scrounging is another variable, and with a little adaptability can be developed into a high art.

For four years, from 1958 to 1962, we lived at Pack Forest, which is a demonstration forest run by Syracuse University College of Forestry. Greg was the assistant forester. I think his title was woods foreman, or something like that. It all came about because we had finally decided that an income of $2,000 per year was just not going to support our ever-growing family. We had five children by then. So we were going to sell our house and property and move to Canada. The Canadian Railroad was looking for people to establish hunting lodges up there, and we had picked out a spot north of Flin Flon, Manitoba.

Well. We had this seventy five acres of nice white

pine, which we needed to sell. It was one of the first certified tree farms in New York State, and Greg was rather proud of it, so he went to see the director of Pack Forest, professor Cliff Foster, to see if he would be interested in buying it. Mr. Foster looked at our seventy five acres and became much more interested in Greg. He said, "You've got really good reproduction going here. We could use a good manager like you. Why don't you come and work for us." The starting salary there was considerably more than $2000 per year, so we decided, much to my relief, not to move any farther north.

We had driven past Pack Forest many times. It's just north of Warrensburg. I had noticed the sign, and thought it must have that name because of the way the trees grew. They were really packed in there. As usual, I was wrong. It was named for Charles Lathrop Pack, who had given the property to Syracuse University to demonstrate proper lumbering prac- tices, and to train foresters. There are Pack Forests in Maine and Washington and two or three other states, as well. The one in New York has about twelve hundred acres. Mr. Pack is buried there.

Every spring the forestry students spent a semester there. They lived in barracks by the lake, and their professors stayed in nearby cottages. All semester they clustered in the woods for lessons and lectures, and did time and motion stud- ies while the regular staff worked in the sawmill or cut pulp- wood to thin out the plantations. The men had great fun reporting to the students with their clipboards, "I'm going to the bathroom now." Or, "Time out for a smoke."

Greg taught one session that he called "Bounty by the Wayside," and all the professors came to watch. They'd been telling their students that when you thinned out the trees, you could probably get twenty-five cents for each little sapling for pulp. Greg would whip out his clippers, trim three branches of a little tree, arrange them artfully into a bunch and twist a wire around them. "There," he'd say, "You've got a swag you can sell to a florist for seventy five cents at Christmas. You can get quite a few from this little tree, and you still have it for pulp." The professors enjoyed that.

This was where we had the squirrels working for us. The plantations had a number of different species of evergreens. In the fall, the squirrels were busy every morning about 6 am cutting off the cones and dropping them. By 7 am they'd gotten them all into neat little piles ready to take away at 8am to store for winter. But at 7:30 am the Gregson kids would come by and kick those cones into baskets. We had one of the best selections of cones in the northeast. They brought three cents apiece at the florist.

Summer is a great scrounging time, as well as early fall. One of those years we found a cranberry bog that yielded up three or four bushels of cranberries. That was the same year that we had picked 120 quarts of blueberries from one handy peak. I never did get very good at cooking up dandelion greens, milkweed, fiddleheads or pigweed, but Greg's mother was good at it. She could make good hand cream using the fat from muskrats, and she had all the kids enjoying sweet fern tea. Much later, one of the boys took a supply of sweet fern with him to college and nearly got arrested, because it looked a lot like pot. He probably did it on purpose, and would have enjoyed the whole thing, except that his van got pretty well demolished while the authorities conducted their search.

I don't know whether you would include hunting and fishing in the scrounge category, but a great many Adirondackers have survived on diets which included a lot of each of those categories. In addition, there are the lichens used for dyeing woolens, if you are so inclined; the birch bark for baskets, picture frames and other decorations; and the odd pieces of misshapen branches and chunks of firewood that make "rustic" furniture.

I dare say the scrounging is pretty good wherever you are, too, but it takes some creative thinking sometimes, and a little desperation always helps. I once taught a class in wreath making, and told my students to bring their own greens, thinking they'd trim a few shrubs or cultivate a gardener somewhere. Wrong again. Having been indoctrinated by city life and commercial florists, my students appeared with scraps from those florists for which they had actually paid. I should have started with a lesson in scrounging.

SECOND COMING

The year was 1969. Both sadder and wiser is what we were. And older. For six years we had been gone from the Adirondacks. I had ironed his crisp white shirts while we tried a different lifestyle. It had not worked. As charming and capable as he was in the "civilized" world, he'd been pining away for his beloved mountains. I had reluctantly become wise enough to know that he needed to get back. That didn't mean I was going peacefully. That's not my style.

It was, after all, only the end of March. Actually, it was April Fool's Day. What a fitting date!

We'd been living most recently in Sullivan County, in southern New York State, on the banks of the Delaware River. Spring had been approaching delicately there. The mountain laurels were beginning to bloom, and the trees were becoming that lovely chartreuse of the early spring season.

We'd been discussing this move for a long time, and I'd been telling him, "It's not spring up there yet, you know. We're moving from this nice warm house to that drafty barn, and I'm going to freeze." There was no point in telling him that he would freeze—he loved cold weather. Besides, he had the kids all sold on the idea. We were going back up there to

"God's Country" and develop a campground on one hundred acres that we were buying. There was only a barn there, and that was where we were going to stay until we got things under way. The kids all thought it was a great adventure.

Greg's father was visiting us from his home in Virginia. "Don't worry," he said, I'll bring you a kerosene heater."

"Oh, sure," I thought, "There goes the central heating again."

It was all excruciatingly true. We did move into that barn on April Fool's Day. There were two feet of snow, and the temperature hovered around zero. I was extremely out of sorts. Greg, on the other hand, was brimming with energy.

The bath

Fortunately for him, the kids were full of energy too. There were five of them. We had left two behind; one in western New York where she'd married a farmer, and one in southern New York where he'd decided to seek his fortune. The five with us were sixteen, fourteen, twelve, seven and five years old. We kept them all busy with the dog sled left over from the last "winteree" that our Boy Scouts had attended. All our belongings had to be brought up from the road on that sled. People always look at me strangely when I tell them we moved in by dog sled. The dog, by the way, was no help at all. He kept getting in the way.

I wouldn't want you to think we were entirely roughing it, though. There was some electricity. And there was a kind of water system. It consisted of a fifty gallon drum up the hill which hooked up to the kitchen sink, and the bathroom sink and toilet. I was not about to go anywhere without a flush toilet. The kitchen sink drained right onto the ground below the floor, but it was all downhill from there.

The bathroom was in the little lean-to addition on the other side of the barn, where there was a bedroom and a bunkroom with two bunks. We had borrowed a little electric heater for the bathroom. Otherwise there was no heat, and there were lots of places where you could see daylight through the walls, but there was a gigantic fireplace. The boys were soon busy up on the hill scrounging firewood with their father, loading it on that sled, and coasting down to the barn. That fireplace consumed cords and cords of wood, and heated maybe a ten foot area around it. My grumbling had reached a crescendo by the time Greg went down the hill and came back with a thing called a salamander. It was a heater that ran on kerosene, or maybe bottled gas, and looked to me like an old vacuum cleaner. It made lots of noise and blew hot air a for-midable distance. All that blowing brought impressive amounts of dust down off the rafters. We developed a ritual. We ran the salamander until we couldn't stand the noise, and then we turned it off until we couldn't stand the cold. I guess the temperature averaged about fifty degrees, at least during the day.

The weather stayed cold and the snow lasted for about a week. Greg was delighted with his acreage. He was out "walking the line" in his snowshoes. The kids were sliding. I stayed in bed under the electric blanket. Every now and then he would show up and tell me what a wonderful day it was. I just grumbled.

This place we moved into had been known as the party barn. It had a good hardwood floor for dancing. There was a twenty-foot high poster at one end advertising El Toro,

Madrid, and there were flags from various cruise ships hanging from the rafters. A screen, covered with menus from those ships separated one corner, which was the kitchen. A large old barber chair sat on the side porch facing the magnificent view. The view really was remarkable. But it did not warm me.

In the kitchen area was an electric range of recent vintage. I spent two days cleaning it before I dared to use it. There had been a mouse nest in the oven, among other things. Finally it was clean so we turned it on, and it immediately exploded. That was dramatic! Apparently the mice had chewed through the wiring. So it was back to the electric frying pan. I got pretty good at one dish meals.

Greg and I had a real bed in the little bedroom. Two boys slept in the bunk room. The five and seven year old had sleeping bags on a mattress by the fireplace, and the oldest boy bunked in another corner. A deep fat fryer became our hot water heater. Baths were a complicated process in a washtub in the bathroom, with the hot water brigade running back and forth, and the bather huddled in there with knees in close proximity to chin.

When we were not shuffling through boxes or stoking the fireplace we played a lot of ping-pong. It was good for keeping warm. Finally it began to warm up outside and then the mud made boots a real necessity. Greg became a little less anxious to slog around his property, and we began planning an upper floor for living quarters, and a prospectus for a campground so we could get funding.

Very soon the sawdust from our balcony-in-progress began to fall into the one-dish meals, giving interesting flavor to the cuisine.

We began a somewhat endless quest to all surrounding banks with maps, diagrams, and carefully chosen figures. Finally in June we found a bank that thought we had a wonderful plan and agreed to finance it. That may have been why Greg forgot to set the brake in the station wagon when we returned home. We watched it coast in a leisurely manner down the hill and over the bank into a ditch. The next day he returned to our financiers and told them how lucky they were to have the first opportunity to also finance the pickup truck and bulldozer we would be needing. He returned in the battered station wagon with a happy grin, so I knew he had succeeded.

At last his father appeared with a real, operational electric kitchen range, and that kerosene heater he'd promised. He was only three months late.

ABOVE AND BEYOND

We called our campground Above and Beyond, because it was. We were located high on the eastern slope of an Adirondack mountain. The altitude was between 1700 and 1800 feet. If you are from anywhere in the far west, this was not really a mountain. It was clearly, merely a high hill. On the other hand, if you were from Long Island or New Jersey, this was impressive. Particularly since there was a view to the east across Schroon Lake, which was down at about 700 feet.

You could practically shake hands with the fire tower on Pharaoh Mountain across the lake. The ridges retreated into the distance, and on a clear day you could see the far off Green Mountains of Vermont. It was a wide view. To the south across the length of the lake, you could lift your eyes to the hills beyond and identify Black Mountain on the far side of Lake George.

The morning mists would settle in the valley and you could imagine walking across a sea of white cotton candy to the misty island peaks rising across the way. Small planes sometimes flew past beneath our deck. It was a heady experience.

As a family, we had previously done a fair amount of

camping during the 50s and 60s, travelling across the United States and Canada, and then being involved with the Boy Scouts of America. So we felt fairly well prepared for this.

That proved wrong.

One problem that we encountered early on was the fact that getting there was an uphill affair. Our camping experiences had been with an eight-cylinder station wagon and a tent trailer, so the hill didn't seem too great an obstacle to us. However, since our modest camping days, progress seemed to have taken over. A large percentage of the camping public was now using equipment spelled with a capital E. This segment was no longer concerned with roughing it. They traveled with trailers wherein were all the comforts of home. An early telephone enquiry was to ask whether we had a dumping station. I had never heard of one and had to be told, before they hung up, that it was a septic system where these trailers could empty their holding tanks, because they were now equipped with bathrooms. We soon acquired a dumping station, and a "honey wagon," and three way hookups, which meant a water spigot for their hose, an outlet for electricity, and a sanitary arrangement for their sewage. We found it hard, however, to lose our rustic atmosphere, and were pleased to be slowly attracting a few hardy souls in tents.

Meanwhile, even the tent trailers were getting larger, and more sophisticated, while cars began to get smaller. It was a three and a half mile climb to our campground from the highway, on a narrow gravel road. Every now and then a small car would appear at our entrance towing a large tent trailer. The driver would usually pop the hood of his car and ask for water for his steaming radiator. It was obvious that he had only come this far because he couldn't find a place to turn around. He would gaze at the uphill driveway to the campground and ask, "How do you get down off this blankety blank hill?" We would never see him again.

Usually the French Canadians traveled a bit lighter. However, we were not their type, either. They would stand on our deck overlooking our magnificent view and ask, "So what's the big attraction here?" Since we didn't really have the party atmosphere they were looking for, we usually sent them on south to Lake George.

There were, nevertheless, a number of hardy souls who stayed with us, snaking their way up into the campground, dodging the trees and jockeying their rigs into impossible places. I recall one Baptist minister who got stuck in one of the sites and had to be extracted. He said he was going to enjoy telling his congregation he'd had difficulties in lofty regions. Except for one forty-foot bus, the largest trailer we encountered was thirty feet long. I was given a tour of this marvelous travelling home with its overstuffed chairs and other luxuries, and was suitably impressed.

We did have one gorgeous, shiny airstream drive up one day. The driver of the Cadillac which towed it allowed his wife to come in and explain that we had too many trees, before they drove off.

Our happiest campers were, of course, the tenters, and we appreciated them. We probably judged everyone by our previous experiences and thought that they were the "real" campers. We even went so far as to construct a few tent platforms. One of these was built over a small stream, and we called it our Frank Lloyd Wright campsite. For the few rustics we had a site far up beyond the regular ones. It was nothing but a clearing, a fireplace and a picnic table. You had to carry in all your supplies and water. It was nicely secluded. But it wasn't used very much. People would call us from New York City insisting that they wanted complete seclusion, and didn't need water or electricity. Usually by the time they got to our entrance they were already more secluded than they had dreamed was possible. We usually wound up giving them a site near the lodge. One couple from Brooklyn found it necessary to leave after only one night. It was just too quiet—and, of course, dark.

Our campers were mostly a cheerful lot, and friendly. You could take a stroll through the campground and usually wind up with two or three cups of coffee, if you could manage that. When we were installing the plastic lining in our new pool, the entire campground turned out to help, and we had a party. There was one site where I could always count on being offered a helping of their stew made of leftovers, which they called Potsareeby. One morning I watched a woman from India making zapatas and she gave me one, stuffed with the previous night's curry. It was very good.

A lot of philosophical discussions were held on that deck overlooking the view, and if anyone had any problems, there was usually someone around with the tools and know-how to fix them. In 1980, after ten years of adventures, joys and sorrows, it was necessary to close the campground, and say goodbye to a whole lot of good friends. They were wild and wonderful people, and I miss them.

WATER, WATER EVERYWHERE, NOR ANY DROP TO DRINK

I live in a little Adirondack town which has a very good water system. I'm told that it's "hard" water, and it does make a deposit on the bottom of the tea kettle, but it tastes very good. And if there's a problem, I call the water commissioner and it gets fixed. All this costs the maximum fee of $75 a year. I consider that a bargain.

It was not always thus.

When I came to the Adirondacks as a new bride, we lived for awhile (as long as we all could stand it) with my husband's parents. They had a well out in the field, with a hand pump that often needed priming. I never did figure out how that worked. Later on, after much digging, there was a well in their basement wherein my father-in-law sometimes kept a mason jar full of money on a string. I don't remember why. I do remember once when he was pulling up the jar it banged on a rock and broke, strewing dollars through the water, but that's another story.

My husband and I soon built our own house over near Chestertown at the site of a former sawmill. There was a lovely cut stone springhouse there that I was told had once served three houses. We kept at least one trout in there. As long as the fish was healthy the spring was supposed to be good. Or maybe it was supposed to keep the bug population down. I never did figure that out either, but Greg certainly enjoyed keeping that fish in there.

The water was gravity fed in a pipe into our basement, and then it had a pump to push it upstairs. I suppose we would not have needed that if we hadn't insisted upon living so high on the hill. Anyway, this pump was another one of those things that stopped working as soon as it was sure that the owner/manager/mechanic/ruler of all things was away. I had received detailed instructions on how to run it. However, I lacked the one essential component known as confidence,

Much later in our many careers, when we lived high up on yet another hill where we intended to establish our commercial campground, we definitely needed a good well. Greg paid a visit to the local extension office to ask the advice of the experts on the location of this well.

They said, "Get a water witch."

You know, of course, that a water witch is a person who uses either a forked stick from a tree, or any of various other devices; metal coat hangers, welding rods, whatever. He is also called a dowser. This water witch will walk your property with this "divining rod" which will twitch in some way to indicate where a vein of water exists underground.

Greg was appalled. He said, "Do you mean to tell me

that modern technology can put men on the moon, but cannot tell me where to drill a well?"

They said, "Get a water witch."

So naturally we went to the well man.

He said, "Where do ya wannit? I cn drill wherever you wannit. Don't make no differnce where."

Of course it made a lot of difference to us, since we were paying him something like fifteen dollars a foot. (This was 1969, you understand.) So one hundred fifty feet later we had our new well, producing six gallons of water per minute. That wasn't much, but Greg figured he could put a thousand gallon tank up at the top of the system, pump the water up there, and gravity feed to everything. If this all sounds a little vague, it's because of my basic lack of understanding. I was not paying close attention. I only needed to have water coming out of the tap when I turned it on.

All this worked out quite well for some time, and then Greg had his second heart attack and died. Sure, we knew he was on borrowed time. This was before bypass surgery, so he had kept taking his medicine and acting like nothing was ever wrong, running up and down the hill keeping campers happy. But his time ran out. There wasn't a lot of time to dwell on it. It was the middle of August and there were still two weeks more of camping season to cope with. Suddenly I had to get acquainted with float valves and pressure tanks and various other details that I'd rather not remember. I learned a lot about water conservation.

By this time there were sixty five campsites, The following season my sons and I approached the crucial Fourth of July weekend with guarded confidence. The weather was sunny and warm. The sites filled up and people were splashing happily in the pool, when the well went dry.

If there'd been anywhere for those two hundred sixty campers to go at this point, I'm sure they would have gone there. As it was, we were stuck with each other. We soon had a bucket brigade in operation. There was a pail of water beside each toilet filled with water from our pond. Since there was no water for showers, the pool stayed pretty busy for awhile. Finally it had to be closed, and all would be swimmers drove off to the beach four miles away. For drinking water, the boys took the pickup truck to a nearby spring and filled fifty-gallon drums. Then they drove around the campground filling all available thermoses, pots, jugs, and any other handy container.

On July 6, a new well man finally came.

He said, "Where do you want it?"

I told him I had no idea.

He set up his drill thirty five feet away from the old well. Soon the campers had a new attraction called watching the well driller. Also listening to the drill. After the first 35 feet, it was bedrock all the way. I'm sure no oil rig ever received more attention. I stayed inside and played solitaire. By the 12th of July, my solitaire had not improved. The few campers we had remaining were rather thoroughly bored with well drilling.

Suddenly my kids came running down the hill followed by a stream of water. We had a gusher! An artesian well! The beaming well man reported a flow of sixty gallons per minute. The new well was three hundred fifty feet deep. Soon we had water flowing to our many faucets, and the pool was back in operation. The laundromat was humming and our grimy campers hit the showers.

The whole operation had only removed our profits for the next two or three years. And did we live happily ever after? Of course not.

Since we were high up on the side of a hill, and since we had a shaft three hundred fifty feet deep filled with water and a metal pipe, guess where the lightning hit? At least once every summer the well man had to come back, pull up the pump, and put in a new one. We could not use plastic pipe. The torque of the heavy-duty pump was too great. An electrician friend surrounded the well with a lightning rod grid. It didn't work. The well man and I became very well acquainted. When I finally closed the campground and sold the place, the new owners found that they could get along quite nicely with the old well, and not worry about lightning.

All that is fine with me. Nowadays if I don't get water coming out of my faucet, I know just what to do. And I hardly even know the water commissioner.

CAN YOU BEAR IT?

The first indication that we might have a problem was a hurried and breathless visit from two of our best campers. They were camping in one of our wilderness sites, quite far out. They wanted us to be the first to know about the bear. They'd been cooking their evening meal of aromatic spaghetti when a real live bear had shown up and taken possession of the whole thing. It seemed to me that in their opinion the loss of a spaghetti dinner was a small price to pay for the privileged encounter they'd just had.

I was happy for them, but apprehensive for us, and with good cause. The next report was from some very disgruntled campers who had returned from town to find their screen room in shreds and their dinner steaks missing. It did not bode well.

Next morning we learned that the bear had torn open a large metal cooler, and was last seen lugging it nonchalantly down the road. When we pointed out our clearly printed instructions to keep all coolers put away in closed vehicles, the injured party said, "But we didn't think you meant our great big heavy one." And of course, the bear couldn't read.

We were always very careful to collect the garbage every evening in an attempt to avoid attracting wildlife, but there always seemed to be some late night diners with exotic garbage. I dare say the bear found the gourmet garbage tastier than berries.

I called the DEC to report all this. I assured them that this bear was terrorizing our campers and inflicting damage. They didn't seem impressed.

The effect on our various campers was rather curious. Those in trailers were enthusiastic. They hung slabs of bacon in the trees and got out their cameras. This was clearly Yogi Bear! Who needed Disney World? Those in tents felt a bit more vulnerable. They were rather subdued. They were likely to awake screaming in the night, pack hurriedly and rush off to civilization.

One night there had been a festive party at one campsite and the celebrants had retired in a happy haze, leaving their site in disarray. Somewhat later the party host awakened to the sound of the bear rummaging through the debris. The camper became incensed and threw his heavy frying pan at the bear, which had looked mildly confused and wandered off. "I can't believe I did that!" he told me next morning.

We had one camper who seemed to think he was in charge of things—especially after he'd had a few cocktails. One evening he took it upon himself to rid us of this problem. With a beer can in one hand and his pistol in the other, he went swaggering off to do away with that bear. I snatched the deer rifle and gave it to my oldest available son who set off after him. They came upon the bear at the far side of the campground, fortunately not in the vicinity of any campsite. Our intrepid hunter was not aware that my son was following him. As he steadied himself to take aim, my son shot over the bear's head. The bear, only mildly annoyed, decided he was unwelcome, and left. The campground became very quiet after that shot. Our hunter friend, pleased with himself, went home to sleep it off.

Finally, after a week of constant phone calls, I was able to convince the DEC that I was not just another hysterical woman. Or else I had become a very agitating thorn in their side. So they sent a trap for the bear. It was a large section of road culvert, with a wall at one end and a door at the other. They baited it with a large slab of bacon, laced with a sedative, slathered with honey, and seared with a blowtorch. It smelled divine. They set it, on its trailer, just beyond the campsites at the perimeter of the campground. As we waited for dusk, I discovered that a large group of trailer campers was planning a campfire vigil out by the trap to watch the fun. By this time I was somewhat out of patience with this segment of the camping public. Despite their speech about how much business they represented to my campground, I vetoed the party.

Surprisingly soon the bear was happily snoozing in the trap, and on its way to more secluded territory. We did not see him again until the following year—same place, same time. Meanwhile we worded our instructions a bit more forcefully. Every now and then a camper would drive in, look around, read our directions, and then very politely decline to stay, saying, "We just can't bear it."

WHEELS III

Around about 1976, I decided to become an art teacher. Never mind that I was already fifty years old, had two children still in school, and no visible means of support. I had a burning desire to get into an occupation which would provide me with a winter income. As I mentioned to my banker when I applied for my annual business loan, I was working on being middle class. He was not amused. I did notice, though, that teachers had paychecks in the winter. I liked that! I'd be one of those.

So I looked around for a college. That was when programs were being developed whereby credit could be given for "life experiences." Goodness knew I'd had "life experience." I envisioned a short college career.

I took a fifty mile jaunt down the road to the nearest one of those places and looked into the matter. Driving into the parking lot in my battered pickup truck, I noticed that all the parking spaces were marked for little sports cars. While I mulled this over, a young coed posted by in her black velvet riding outfit on an attractive horse, and it became clear to me that I was not going to fit in here. It turned out that this was an accurate assessment. My credentials did not fit their program, which was also expensive. Next, I looked into a college that only required that you work with a mentor and report in periodically. Unfortunately, my experience didn't fit their requirements either, and it was also expensive.

So I did the obvious thing. I signed up at the nearest junior college and started at the beginning, like any other freshman.

Then I looked for some cheap transportation. The junior college was forty miles away, and my old pickup truck didn't get very good mileage. So I got a used little green Volkswagen. I also got a book on how to take care of a VW. Self sufficiency was what I had in mind. I should have known better.

That was the year I invested in fur lined boots. Apparently Germany doesn't get very cold. VW's are well known for faulty heaters, and mine never did manage to get warm. Also, I never did discover how to keep the windshield defrosted during a sleet storm without simply pulling over every half mile or so, and applying defrosting solution from a spray can.

It had a strange gearshift, but that was not as strange as the fact that the motor was way off in the back. I guess the manufacturer decided that it was such a light little tin can of a car the weight would give it better traction back there. The real shocker, though, was when I parked it at the college one dark morning and forgot to turn off the headlights so the battery died. After locating the college custodian with jumper cables, we spent a great deal of time looking for the battery. Imagine our surprise at finding it under the back seat! Volkswagens are all put together with nuts and bolts made according to the metric scale. They require a particular kind of mechanic. The one I found was just as odd as the machine itself. I spent untold hours sitting in his garage doing my studying while he fussed and fumed over my little car. Occasionally he would become frustrated and throw an offending part off into the woods. He often explained to me the various idiosyncrasies of the vehicle and advised me to adjust my requirements to suit its limitations. Since I was in no position to replace it, I tried to be understanding.

It was during this time that I became the district director for the New York State Parent Teacher Association. That little green Volkswagen took me all over the Adirondacks while I tried to service a small handful of PTA units. It was a three hour drive from one corner to the other of my territory. One evening I was travelling along Route 11 west of Plattsburgh when a large dog ran out in front of me and I hit it. Fortunately, the dog survived. But after that my right fender was bent just enough so that its headlight seemed to be searching for another dog. I'm quite sure that whenever I showed up in downtown Amsterdam or Binghamton or Rochester or Buffalo in my little green Volkswagen, quite a few of the good PTA people were embarrased to know me.

By the time I transferred to a four year college in Albany, the little green Volkswagen was all worn out, and my

#1 son acquired for me a recently refurbished VW station wagon. This one had something called fuel injection. I got well acquainted with that because it seemed to leak a lot. I had to find a new mechanic, too, since I was now renting in Malta. Big city mechanics were expensive, so I prayed a lot. Also, I joined the AAA. That was handy, especially when I locked my keys inside. One time I limped into a service station with a problem, and the attendant came out to have a look. When he saw what I was driving, he looked at me in disgust and said, "Lady, we only work on cars here."

That was the car I was driving one day when I had to attend a meeting in Syracuse. I started out bright and early from Schroon Lake and the alternator died in Saratoga. A very nice service station man there told me how to manage it. "Just don't turn off the motor for any reason," he said, "until you get to a garage in Syracuse. Park it there and have them charge the battery for you."

I followed slow hay wagons and hesitated at red lights praying the motor wouldn't stall, all the way to Syracuse. After the meeting I broke a few speed limits hurrying home before it got too dark. It was an interesting trip.

Finally in 1980 I graduated with a degree in art education. At the time, there was just one opening in the entire state for an art teacher, so I went to New Zealand with my mother. She'd waited thirty five years to give me a graduation present, and this was it. When I got back, I found that the VW had been demolished in an accident. Was I sad? Was I angry? Not hardly. I bought a used Plymouth with only 100,000 miles on its odometer. I have never driven a VW again.

THE SUMMER JOB

It is something of an enigma that the short Adirondack summer, which all of us Adirondackers look forward to all year, is the time when most of us are almost too busy to notice it going by. The saving grace is that our two-month jobs give us enough to remember and talk about for the next ten.

For two or three summers I had a fascinating job at a nearby attraction called Frontier Town. The tourists would come and tour the place where, among lots of other things, a grist mill was grinding corn meal, a team of oxen was grinding hemlock bark for the tanning factory, a goat was walking a treadmill to wash the clothes, and a weaver was weaving a blanket on a barn loom. I was hired as a weaver. The shop was right across from the dunking pond, and every day the Marshall would bring in one of the bad guys who robbed the train, and Judge Roy Bean would give him a really short trial, and he'd get dunked. Then there'd be a shootout on the main street, just outside the saloon, and Speedy Gonzales would get outdrawn and gunned down. The stagecoach would be unsuccessfully raided by Indians, and the Pony Express rider would report trouble on the trail, whereupon the Marshall would swear in all the little kids to join the cavalry and they'd get marched up to the fort for basic training. I can still see the Marshall telling those kids, "Raise your right hand—no, the other right hand." There was also a rodeo and an Indian Powwow, and a big fat bear to feed.

The weavers' shop was run by an ancient little lady called Mrs. Hanneford. She was the widow of a famous clown, and in years past had toured Europe with the circus. She was at least 99 years old, and built entirely of steel. She sized me up when I came to work and was visibly unim-pressed. She said, "If you're going to work here you'll have to learn to spin." I considered myself a pretty good weaver, but spinning was not my thing. She gave me a drop spindle and a book, and said, "Go learn." Three days and many tears later, I was a spinner. By the end of the summer I was demonstrating spinning with the drop spindle, the walking wheel, and the travelling wheel. I was carding and spinning and using the clock wheel and the niddy-noddy.

On good days, some of us would go out in the yard and cook up a batch of dye in the big cauldron over a good fire. We had our pictures taken a lot in our flowered dresses and big aprons and dust caps while we dyed skeins of wool with goldenrod to a nice brassy yellow. On cold days I kept the little box stove stoked with wood. My patter was almost as good as Mrs. Hanneford's. She would tell the tourists all about spinning and weaving. Sometimes it was the truth, but it was always entertaining. I tried to be more accurate, but it was her show. I was busy thumping along on that barn loom.

Every now and then, one of those Canadian visitors would lean across and tell me about his or her grandmother weaving rag rugs. One man taught me a good weaver's knot.

At noon we'd go next door to the homestead and bum a cup of pea soup from Dot Liberty who'd been cooking it over the fire since early morning. When I got my coffee break, I'd wander over to the gristmill and get some freshly ground corn meal to take home. Later on they wrote me into the afternoon show. Every day at 2 p.m. I got my broom and went over to the saloon where I beat the drunkard with it, all the while yelling at him, "Go home, you drunken fool!" and other choice phrases. Then he'd wander out into the street and get shot.

About half an hour before closing time, Mrs. Hanneford would decide she'd done enough for one day, and she would sit down at the rug loom and stare stonily into space. She never wove anything. It was not in her repertoire. The rest of us would hustle to please the customers. Presently the farewell music would come from the loudspeakers, and she would disappear down the trail. We'd close the shutters and lock the door and wander up the winding trail out of there to the strains of "God Be With You Till We Meet Again." It always felt just like emerging from Brigadoon. I wore my period costume through the supermarket on the way home and enjoyed the curious stares.

Those were good summers. Since then I've gone on to other summer jobs. Frontier Town changed hands a few times and then closed. Like so many other Adirondack stories, that one is done. I saved one of the shawls I wove there. Whenever I get it out, I can almost hear that song again..."God Be With You Till We Meet Again."

The Tree

THESE TREES

Outside my bedroom window is a very large tree, and it's easy to imagine that I'm in the middle of it. I wake up in the morning and look through its thick branches to find the sun. Birds and squirrels are busy out there, and it's something like living in a tree house.

In winter the twigs often sparkle with ice, and the snow piles up on the broad, mossy limbs. In spring, the grey catkins hang, and fall softly to make a fluffy grey carpet on the walk. In summer the grey-green leaves turn inside out to warn of rain, and in the fall it takes two or three sessions of raking by platoons of grandchildren to get rid of all of them. The tree's roots are everywhere, and little baby trees are constantly trying to take over the gardens.

It's a poplar tree—or, as a true Adirondacker would say, a popple. It took me two or three weeks, when I moved here, to find out what kind of tree it is. I'm not an authority on these things. My husband was the real authority.

I didn't really know how ignorant I was until the first spring after he died, when I decided to tap the maple trees again and boil some syrup. I found the spigots and a hammer, but couldn't find the snowshoes, so I went wallowing out through the snow. Eventually I stood hip deep in snow, confronting a towering tree. Gazing up into its branches, it slowly dawned upon me that I had no idea whether or not it was a maple tree. I looked around at this great collection of trees and realized that there was no chance that I would know where to put that spigot. I could tell you what a cedar or pine or hemlock or spruce was, and which was balsam fir. Their needles were self explanatory. But after that I was lost. My maple sugaring days were over.

Greg had been a forester. We had taken long walks through the woods while he pointed out which species were being attacked by various diseases. I was always amazed, after these walks, to find so many trees still standing around looking healthy. One of his various business ventures involved cutting and shipping cedar poles. He had cutting rights on a large tract of land bordering the forest preserve, and spent the greater part of one winter there. Every night he would return with more tales about the herd of deer that followed him around cleaning up the twigs and bark from the cedar.

Our own seventy five acres became one of the first certified tree farms in New York State. We were both rather proud of that. In 1958 he became the assistant forester at Pack Forest, a 12,000 acre demonstration forest located near Warrensburg. One of his duties there was to give tours to interested foresters. I was constantly amazed at his expertise.

A few of his casual lessons actually stuck with me, but

only a few. I know, for instance, that birch bark will always burn, even in the rain, because it's full of oils. This is handy if you need to start a fire. And if you can't get seasoned wood for your fireplace, the thing to get is ash. Don't let anyone sell you pine for burning, though. Softwoods make quite a blaze, but they burn quickly, and you'll spend all your time feeding the fire. I suppose you already know that generally speaking, the soft woods are the evergreens, and the deciduous are hardwoods. You knew that, didn't you? And the difference between a full cord and a face cord of wood?

So whenever I want to impress my city friends with my woodsy expertise, I casually drop a few of these little gems, carefully avoiding getting into any detail.

Of course, some things I learned the hard way. For instance, you don't use birch for fence posts. Birch is very brittle and will soon rot. It will only look good for about one season. And never use a stick from a pine tree to cook your marshmallow. It will taste really bad. Not even as good as cough syrup. Trust me—I tried it.

When I became an art teacher, one of my favorite lessons at Christmas was to make prints of cedar—usually with white paint on red or green paper. They looked like little Christmas trees on cards or wrapping paper. The little kids always enjoyed that. In addition to the cedar, I usually brought in some pine, balsam fir, spruce and hemlock. Then we'd have a game of identification.

Of course, in the fall, we'd use gorgeously colored

maple leaves and learn about mixing colors. In the winter we'd learn about perspective and pattern, using the stark, bare branches of the trees seen from the art room windows.

Out of my kitchen window, I have been watching a pine tree grow. It started out during one of those summers when I couldn't get the lawn mower started. It was a foot high by the time that lawn got mowed, and I staked it out so it wouldn't get clipped. By next summer it will be five feet high. There are two huge old dying spruces north of my house that are parents to a large nursery of little spruce trees. The amazing ability of nature to constantly replenish the landscape is a constant wonder to me. I have read about the vast harvest of hemlock for the tanneries here, less than one hundred years ago, and I have seen pictures of barren hillsides, but I can take a walk through that same landscape and find it hard going among the wealth of trees.

When spring comes, though, before the leaves appear, I can't possibly tell you which are the maple trees. But that's all right. I have a good friend with a large sugar bush, who does all that sugaring and keeps me supplied with syrup. I could go on with this, but I seem to have acquired a real hunger for pancakes. Maybe later.

MY COUSIN, THE BAT LADY

I'm sure that everyone has illustrious relatives, and I am certainly no exception. Actually, the relative I want to tell you about is my husband's cousin, but I have adopted her because she's a fascinating lady. She's a retired teacher and usually lives in New York City, which is nice for me when I want to catch a bit of city life. I can go there and spend days in the museums and nights at the theatre and enjoy her company all at once. She taught overseas for a time in the Near East and Africa, and climbed Kilimanjaro, among other things, and has many stories to tell. She also has a summer home in the Adirondacks not too far from my own, so we see each other often enough to keep up on what's going on.

The other night, we encountered each other at Seagle Colony, the summer school of music in Schroon Lake, where we watched a great performance of "A Little Night Music." During the intermission she regaled us with the latest report on her bats. Her home was built about fifteen years ago and finished with what we call "waney-edge" siding, a horizontal siding made of pine planks with the bark left on one edge, and usually finished with a dark stain. The fellow who did the job was apparently cutting corners. He didn't overlap the planks very well, they were not suitably dried, so that they shrank, and he used the wrong nails. The result is a wall well suited as a habitat for bats. The little critters only need about a quarter of an inch opening to crawl into and make themselves at home.

In addition, the mason who built her fireplace and the man who did the roof were apparently not on speaking terms, because there are gaps where the chimney goes through the roof that allow entrance to the bats, and they have certainly taken advantage of the opportunity.

I'm sure we can all agree that bats have their place in the natural scheme of things, but that does not include inside a house.

This cousin of mine is no shrinking violet. She has put up with this bat population for a number of seasons, but she said it's really beginning to bother her. "For one thing," she said, "it's gotten so that nobody wants to come visit me anymore."

She used to have a Welsh Terrier who loved to do battle with the little critters, but he finally died. Now she has a new terrier who is much more sedate, doesn't appreciate the opportunity for adventure, and is most often located under the bed.

We were listening politely to this report, but when she mentioned being up two or three times every night with these bat incidents we started to pay more attention. She noted that it was really disconcerting to be dive-bombed incessantly, and

150

described one incident when she flailed away with her bad-
minton racket at a bat which had taken cover under her pillow.
"I banged away at it," she said, "and it seemed to come apart.
That's when I realized that it was a mother bat and her baby. I
felt like a murderer."

This lady is an avid naturalist. She tried noise
machines, but they didn't seem to make much difference.
Now she's taking a series of shots to prevent rabies, because
she figures constant exposure to these bats can be pretty
chancy. She assured us that the shots didn't hurt very much at
all.

Her total bat fatalities for the season, she said, were
about 27 so far, and the season's young.

I am thinking back to my own experiences with bats,
and it's been pretty sketchy. I definitely don't have my
cousin's tolerance. A long while ago, when I still had a husband and we lived for awhile in a barn, my attitude toward
bats was fairly cavalier. We had a resident bat who kept us
regularly entertained. We called him Sam. My sons' girlfriends were somewhat unnerved by him, and I must admit
that I rather enjoyed their discomfort. But there was only one
of him, he never seemed to multiply, and we had him outnumbered. And I knew I could count on the man of the house, my
husband, in case of emergency.

Some time after my husband died, I remember corner-
ing a bat on a wall, one night, and summoning all my nerve to
cover it with a metal mixing bowl. Then I had one of my

long-suffering children slide a cookie sheet under it, we opened the door, and threw the whole ensemble out into the night. I did a lot of shaking afterward.

So you can see I'm not well suited to cohabitate with bats, and will be happy to merely listen for reports from my cousin, the bat lady. Meanwhile, I will probably be among those who politely decline visits to her lovely summer home. I imagine it's a great place, though, for those who have had it with small flying insects.

WILD ANIMALS I HAVE KNOWN

It was a fellow named Seton, I think, who wrote a book with this title. It was one of my husband's favorite books. I can't do a whole book about them. My exposure to animals, both wild and domestic has been somewhat limited. That's the way I like it.

There was the skunk I met up with one dark and rainy night in early spring when my pickup truck got stuck in a mud hole, and I had to get out and walk. It was only a mile or so to my in-law's house. By the time I got there my eyes had grown accustomed to the dark so it was easy to see the little critter with the big white stripe down its back, guarding their path. When we got through staring at each other, we each went our separate ways, having treated each other with all due respect.

Then there were the three racoons roosting in the birch tree right outside our house one night. Greg got me out of bed to see them. I stood there shivering in my bare feet while they stared down at us in stony silence. They were gone in the morning.

Years later, when I was running a campground up on

the side of an Adirondack hill, we had an ongoing problem with racoons rattling around among the garbage cans making messes. My boys, who were pretty well grown by then, decided to alleviate the problem. It was their opinion that those racoons were state property. One night they trapped those bothersome critters in some empty garbage cans, loaded them onto the pickup truck and took them down the hill to the state campground, five miles away, and left them there. That was so successful, they kept it up until we were pretty well rid of the problem. Years later I was tooling past the state campground on my way home and struck a racoon so big I thought it had damaged the car. Fortunately, the bumper was a sturdy one. But evidently the state takes good care of its racoons.

We had quite a few wild critters at our campground. In winter the chickadees could be counted upon to eat out of our hands if we stood very still. The squirrels enjoyed the birdseed, too, and entertained us with their antics. One squir-rel developed a maverick tooth growing up the side of its face and endangering its eye, so we borrowed a have-a-hart trap and caught him in it with the intention of helping him out. He was terrified, and kept clawing at the wires with his teeth, so we got the clippers and clipped off that tooth. When we opened the trap, he was out of there like a shot. We never saw him again. Another squirrel I recall was the flying squirrel that was into the breads and cookies in our camp store. We knew who it was, because one night we happened to gaze at the deer head over the fireplace and there he was, looking at us from between its horns. As we watched, he took a flying leap, soared gracefully onto a lamp, bounced off onto the counter top, then to a stool and finally the floor. He disappeared before we could see where he went. Next morning we had him in that trap and returned him to the wild.

We tried raising a few rabbits at the campground, but campers' dogs were forever getting loose and climbing into the cages looking for dinner, and eventually all those rabbits had taken cover in the great outdoors. One mother rabbit had a brood of bunnies in a hole beneath a boat that one camper had stored at his site. After a few weeks the camper arrived from the city bringing his two poodles. That mother rabbit successfully terrorized those poodles, who took cover under their master's bed until the baby rabbits were weaned and the mother moved out. Meanwhile, I was doing a great business selling carrots to delighted kids who were gathered in clumps all over the lawn feeding little rabbits. The rabbits were enthusiastic about those carrots, and would sometimes keep nibbling right up the kids' fingers, so I kept the bandaids handy. One afternoon I was kidding with a chubby boy while I bandaged his finger.

"Now, don't faint," I said, and he dropped like a stone.

Those rabbits lasted in the wild for about two seasons.

Porcupines are big clumsy animals who will chew on most anything, especially if there's salt on it, and nail all nosey dogs with those nasty quills. The dogs never seem to figure out what the problem is, and require numerous lessons. A large porcupine has been known to cause such confusion among inexperienced hunters that it's been mistaken for a bear and shot. At one Boy Scout show, Greg's Explorers exhibited a caged porcupine with a sign explaining that they are good food for survival in the wilderness. They waxed poetic. The signs read,

"A tap on the snout will knock him right out" and

"It will stick to your gullet if you just don't smell it"

I can't tell you what the public's reaction was. I was in the hospital having our fourth child at the time.

By the way, if any of you hunters should actually shoot a bear, I would advise you to do it near a road. A friend of ours shot one about three miles into the woods, and it took five men all day to drag it out. It was a fat old thing, and settled into every little hole they came to. They hung it in his yard, and his beagle barked wildly all afternoon. We took some pictures of it. They told me the meat tasted a lot like pork, but after I got a strong whiff of it's aroma my apetite was gone. It became a bearskin rug that his children enjoyed for many years.

I have heard that deer hunting has declined in these parts because there has been a population explosion of coyotes. I am no authority on such matters. My only experience with coyotes was the dead one I found on my lawn recently. Apparently it had been hit by a car during the night. It looked to me rather like a mangy dog, so I supposed it was a coyote.

It was certainly not a fox. I called the local game warden and told him there was this dead body on my lawn. Then I paused while trying to think whether it was really a coyote. During that pause, the poor man apparently thought I was referring to a human and got quite excited. I had to do a lot of apology and explanation. He was very nice and came and took it away.

So. There are those who think that perhaps if we were to re-introduce the wolf to the Adirondacks they would some-how replace a lot of these mangey coyotes. I'm not sure what that's supposed to do for the deer population. It occurs to me that if nature doesn't get tampered with too much everything works out naturally. But of course, I'm no authority.

A few years ago the DEC talked about reintroducing the moose to the Adirondacks. It was said that there used to be moose in these parts and it would be nice to have them back. Now there's an impressive animal! I remember reading about one of the old Adirondack guides who claimed to have shot the last moose about 1865. He said he couldn't under-stand why there weren't any more moose. "Why, I can remember," he said, "when I shot a good sixty of them in one year." There were also reports that they were done in by a parasite that got into their brains and killed them. Apparently the parasite incubated in the deer population without affecting the deer.

About the time that this reintroduction was being pro-posed, for only three million dollars, there were sightings of moose being reported. By 1996 there were said to be 30 moose in the Adirondacks. I couldn't help wondering why there had to be such a rush to hurry things along. I wrote to the DEC and suggested that perhaps they might be interested in reintroducing the beaver to Delmar. I understand a lot of DEC people live in Delmar, which is a fashionable suburb of Albany. I mentioned that the beaver used to be plentiful there, and people should not be denied the pleasure of their company. I told them I knew a number of local landowners who would be happy to thin out their beaver population and send them there for relocation. For some reason, the DEC never answered my letter.

Now that I'm supposedly retired, I don't get much contact with animals any more. My kids keep telling me I should have a cat to keep down the mouse population explosion in my basement every fall, but they don't fool me. They're just looking for some place to farm out their surplus kittens. Besides, quite by accident, I've discovered the better mousetrap! What you do is you leave the lid off the big garbage can down there. Those mice get curious. They climb out on an overhanging shelf and drop right in. There's no way out. So far I've removed four or five dead bodies- mouse bodies, that is. That's enough wild life for me.

JANUARY PETITION

I am about to circulate a petition to do away with January. Can you think of a more unnecessary month? Aside from the bitter cold here in the northeast, there are all those annual bills. I'm not even talking about Christmas credit card catastrophes. There are real estate taxes, and car insurance, and house insurance and heating bills, among other things.

You might advise me to spend January in Florida, as so many from these parts do, but that's no guarantee there will be warmth. I've been there in both December and February, and nearly frozen. Floridians don't invest all that much in central heating, so they're vulnerable to every little cold snap. Besides, I've developed a real dislike for that state. For one thing, there is a large population of old ladies with blue hair, and they're beginning to look a lot like me. I wouldn't want to get lost in that shuffle. As one of the local gendarmes down there confided to me one day, "Old people in Florida are a dime a dozen." And what a population! It is obvious that the whole state is slowly sinking under it all. Just notice how high the other corner of the continent is. They're really tipping the boat!

But I digress. We were discussing January. I haven't

always had this aversion. It probably began about twenty years ago on January 16, when I went to a PTA meeting. I didn't want to go. The temperature was thirty five degrees below zero. But I was the chairman.

Then various of my teenage children had an audition for their band in Lake George. I bet you thought Lake George disappeared in the winter! So they loaded up their equipment from the basement and left, forgetting to close the outside door. When I returned, everything was frozen pretty solid. The next week, during the January thaw, there was major plumbing taking place at our house.

After that, for a number of years I gritted my teeth and walked softly until after January 16. I won't dwell upon the annual disasters. I developed quite an unreasonable complex about it.

These past few years things were calming down somewhat. Catastrophic events were distributing themselves hither and yon, and I was beginning to relax a bit about January. That was a mistake. Last year I spent the whole month holed up with complications from a hospital stay. I was pretty much confined to quarters and lost a lot of weight, which would have been a happy experience except that while my figure improved my face did not. Gaunt is a word that comes to mind.

Then this January—on the seventeenth, even—I went shopping. It was a lovely clear day. I was striding confidently across the parking lot at the mall, and found the only patch of ice for miles around. In about half a second, I was lying on a broken arm on the pavement. Most undignified. I was hauled off to the emergency room and handed from one technician to another, and given codeine, which left me in a sleepy haze while I waited for my daughter to come and take me away.

As it turned out, I'm allergic to codeine. I developed a full body rash to go with everything else. My unfortunate daughter had to get me up and put me to bed, shower me, cut

Aint cold, are ya?

my meat, administer medication, and give me a driving lesson so I could go home a month later. My friends had to ferry me from doctor to doctor to doctor. I must confess that sitting in waiting rooms watching the array of crutches, braces, wounds and slings made me feel relatively healthy.

I didn't intend to give you all these gory details, but they are still so fresh in my mind. My doctor seems to think I'll be all right by July.

So that's my beef about January. I'm sure you must have two or three that you could add, and you'll want to add your name to this petition. I try to face these things with bravery and courage, but by January 31 I'm pretty well defeated. That's another thing. I notice February has the decency not to last so long.

TV

I enjoy television. Don't you? It keeps you up to date on things, and when you've had a long hard day coping, you can usually find something on there that you can coast through without any effort. You don't even have to react. There are laugh tracks that will do that for you. Even when it's not funny. But you must admit it gives you coverage of momentous occasions in history. The Kennedy assassination comes to mind.

My grandchildren mostly think that TV came along with Adam and Eve, and they don't really believe me when I tell them there once wasn't any. We got our first television in 1956. That was the year we were expecting our fifth child, and we needed to put an addition on the house. Two bedrooms were hardly adequate any more. And Eric, our number 2 child, needed his tonsils removed. All this made it necessary to renegotiate our mortgage, so we included the price of a television set.

That was a momentous decision. We didn't realize just how momentous until we turned it on. For two or three weeks thereafter we were bleary eyed from sleep deprivation. There was the Ed Sullivan show, and Edward Murrow, and Dinah

Shore, and Jack Parr, and Milton Berle and Imogene Coca and Jack Benny and I Love Lucy, and Playhouse 90. It was exhausting.

When the new baby came we propped him up in front of the screen right along with the rest of us to watch the world go by. Television reception was a challenge among the Adirondack hills, and Greg rose to that challenge often, putting up antennas, installing rotors and repairing wires. The TV went with us on various moves, and he did his high wire act for stations in Rochester and Buffalo and New York City. In 1969, when we finally returned to the Adirondacks, that old black and white TV was still with us, complete with all the scratches and gouges and the hole in its side where it had gotten punched when it refused to function in the middle of the Army/Navy football game.

By 1973 that old Dumont was seventeen years old and it graced the lodge at our campground on a northeast slope in the Adirondacks. We were enjoying stations from Burlington, Vermont, and Poland Springs, Maine. Our television had become a noteworthy antique; a conversation piece. People would gaze at it transfixed. They'd poke each other and say, "Wow! A black and white TV!"

1973 was the year Greg died. It seemed to me that a great many things didn't work very well after that. The old TV got so it would only function sporadically. It had so many accumulated idiosyncrasies I didn't turn it on very much any more. The horizontal hold would give up right in the middle of things, so that the actors seemed to be forever rolling their eyes, and snow would be falling right in the middle of Gilligan's Island. I finally sent it to the repair shop for another go-round.

After a few weeks, I remembered that the TV was gone and called the repair shop. The fellow there was an old friend of ours. I asked him whether the TV was fixed yet. He said, "Oh, was I supposed to fix that? I sent it off to the dump a long time ago."

I said, "Look, Louie, I know it was not much of a set, but it was the only one I had. What am I supposed to do now?"

So he sold me a used color TV, and I hardly missed the antique conversation piece any more.

Since then I have acquired TVs the same way I've acquired most of my furniture. Somebody was getting a new one, so I got the old one. I've been doing very well that way. All my things have real character. Then one Christmas my children decided I needed a VCR, and after that the cable company came by. They have a strange collection of stations, but there are lots of them. I can count on my grandchildren to make everything work, so I reckon I'm ready for the twenty first century.

Now, I have heard rumors about something called digital TV, but I figure if I'm lucky I won't need to grapple with that until the great grandchildren are ready to take over.

I DON'T DO MATH

It must be that I am pretty much totally right brain oriented, because I have no aptitude for figures. This became evident at a fairly early age. The only math I understood particularly well in school was Geometry. I think it was because it involved drawings, so that I could pretty well see what was happening. My father was a builder, and I often spent hours with his house plans playing house, moving imaginary people from room to room. I was eighteen before I discovered that there were people who could not read blueprints, but I am still in awe of those who can do square root. Algebra is too abstract. Calculus is a mystery.

At age eighteen I became a draftsman, and I was advised to take a class in trigonometry. It was fascinating. The problem was that I hardly ever got the right answer. I lasted just three weeks. Clearly, my future did not lie in this direction.

Large numbers are confusing. After the first two commas I tend to get lost. I'm never sure how many thousands of dollars anything is. 8,000 or 80,000? My memory bank gets overloaded. Fortunately it's irrelevant. I'll never be rich enough for it to matter.

I once decided to reinforce some wooden railings on our long deck by adding a network of rope strung on hundreds (thousands?) of screw eyes. When a friend found me struggling with the installation of these millions of screw eyes, standing on my head, cramping my tired and bloody fingers, he got his electric drill and came to my rescue. I now had little screw eyes every three inches top and bottom, having bought up all the screw eyes between Albany and Plattsburgh.

Then I measured carefully and calculated tediously before I took the forty mile trip to the hardware store in my little green Volkswagen. Collaring a clerk there, I said, "I need 12,000 yards of quarter inch manila rope."

He looked at me strangely. "Are you sure?" he asked.

I was definite. "Yes, 12,000 yards."

He pondered. Finally he took me to the storeroom where boxes were stacked against the wall. Indicating this wall of boxes he told me, "That's 12,000 yards of manila rope."

I considered this matter, visualizing the size of my VW. "Do you suppose," I ventured, "that I meant feet?"

As I paid for my two boxes of rope and turned to leave, I could hear the clerk telling his next customer, "You see that lady there with the rope? You know what she asked for?"

Finally I became an art teacher. My students were all trained to know that they should check their marks at the end of the semester. I was able to save face with them by drawing

168

little diagrams on the board proving that one and one make three. My point was that it all depends on your point of view, and that all things are possible in art. It was great for my ego.

I manage fractions pretty well by visualizing pies. Rulers are wonderful. They have increments that can be counted until your space is all used up!

Percentages are a constant surprise, especially when adding interest to my debts. But you needn't worry about me. I can balance my check book—at least when it's one month at a time. And if I have trouble with my income tax I just call the IRS and let them worry about it.

Meanwhile I don't worry too much until someone mentions a thing called bottom line. Then I tend to go all to pieces.

SNAKE EYES

SNAKE EYES

In 1984, I received tenure as a teacher, and decided it was probably safe to find a place to live closer to where I worked. I had known for quite awhile that I couldn't afford the upkeep on that big barn where I'd lived for the past fifteen years. Now that the children were all grown and gone, and there was only one of me, all I needed was a little house. I'd been driving past this one for three years, thinking it looked rather lonely, and wondering whether it was large enough to have a bathroom. So finally I got up the nerve to find out, and it did.

Fortunately the place was inexpensive. Not only did I not have much money, but also what little I had would be needed for repairs. My #2 son had inspected it with me and said, "Oh sure, we can fix it up alright." After the deal was done, my #5 son came along and had a look, and said, "What, are you crazy?'

My #3 son moved in with me, and it was a good thing that he did, because he was handy with wiring, among other things. The toaster and electric mixer would not both work at the same time, because there wasn't enough electricity. He had to install new wiring and control panel, and play host to the electric inspector.

The basement floor was dirt—mud, actually, in the spring, and the whole house was standing on a sea of two by fours stationed on little stone islands down there. One day, #2 and #5 sons showed up with quantities of cement, and laid a basement floor with a nice trench around the outside edge to accommodate the spring runoff. Then #4 son came and repaired the stone walls down there. After that, various sons came and juggled with jacks and cedar posts and stone piers until the house stood fairly level. During their operations, the rocking motions in the upper regions of the house were almost enough to bring on seasickness. Finally I had a basement interesting enough for me to refer to it as my wine cellar. My #1 son even came and built a sturdy outside basement door to replace the canvas flap that had been there.

That seemed like a pretty good pausing place. I didn't really mind that there were no basement steps. There was a judiciously placed step ladder if you wanted to go down there. I didn't really need to. The washer and dryer down there weren't hooked up yet, and who knew when that would happen? All that jockeying had created a little crack where the bathroom wall met the tub, but we'd get to it.

So I settled into my work routine, and my resident son settled into his.

One afternoon I came home from school and headed to the bathroom. There, in the bathtub was a very live snake. I cautiously backed out and shut the door. There was no way I was going in there with that snake.

"Now, wait," I told myself. "Let's think. There must be someone who will remove that snake for you."

I went to the phone and called my #4 son who lived right next door. His wife answered. He wasn't home. "Well," I said, "When he comes back, would you send him over? There's a snake in my bathtub." I didn't wait for her reaction.

I hung up and thought some more. That snake was assuming large proportions. My #5 son was working on a job just eight miles away. Surely he'd come and save me. I called.

"Lance," I said, "Can you come over for a minute?"

"Whatsamatter, Maw," he asked. "I'm pretty busy."

"Well, uh, there's a snake in my bathtub."

"Well, crimunnee. Take him out, why doncha?"

"I'm not about to have anything to do with that snake," I said. "And I need to go to the bathroom."

"Aw, Maw, don't be such a baby. I'm busy."

I hung up. Ungrateful wretch. I used to change his diapers, and he won't even come to my rescue. By this time that snake was at least a boa constrictor. Also by this time I really needed to use a bathroom. I called my very good friend, who lived only five miles away.

"Fran," I said, "May I use your bathroom?"

"Sure you can. What's the trouble?"

"Well, uh, there's a snake in my bathtub."

She laughed. This bosom buddy of mine just laughed

and laughed. It was exasperating. She obviously had no concept of my predicament. I stood there trying to think of a cutting remark, and then I noticed somebody riding up on a bicycle. It was my #5 son, after all, coming to my rescue.

"Never mind," I told her icily, and hung up.

Lance came strolling in, grabbed a paper towel and headed for the bathroom. Moments later he reappeared with the snake, maybe 12 or 15 inches long, holding it carefully just behind its head.

"Did you ever notice," he remarked, "how they have a really funny smell when they're scared?"

As he headed out the door with it, his brother from next door appeared, with a friend in tow, because he too was afraid of snakes. They were both relieved to find that the problem was already solved, and everybody had a good laugh at my expense.

After that incident, every time I took a bath I kept a wary eye on the little gap in the wall, watching for little beady eyes. Next vacation I took a trip. While I was away, my various sons came and put in a new floor in my kitchen and bathroom, mainly because my refrigerator was beginning to fall through. They discovered that the sill was rotted in back of the bathtub, and replaced it. They also found evidence of a nest of snakes living in the wall there. I came home to a nice new floor, and a tight new wall around the bathtub. The boa constrictor is now just another uncomfortable memory. I hope it stays that way.

RAIN FOREST

This is a steaming jungle. Here it is the middle of
summer and you have to wear boots in the mornings whether
it has rained or not, Maybe it's that way in lots of places, but
I've lived here so long I've forgotten. And you know, now that
I think of it, there's always something falling on your head,
too. If not rain or snow, then catkins, blossoms, sap from the
pines, cones from the spruces or leaves from the maples.
Besides that, in my lumpy yard you need to push your way
through sumac, milkweed, giant dandelions, and wild things
of every description. Nature keeps taking over, defying all
attempts at dignity and order.

Now and then I try a garden. It is futile. As soon as I
plant seeds, one of two things immediately occurs: 1. We have
another frost, and/or 2. It stops raining. By the time we are
back to a normal drizzle, I've forgotten what I planted. I wait
hopefully to see greenery of some sort, and then I watch carefully to see what that greenery turns into. By the time I've figured out which of those green things are weeds, they've
crowded out whatever it was that I planted. And one does not
get a second chance in this climate.

So I have largely given up on trying to cultivate a garden. Instead I cultivate the gardeners. They seem to have some sort of instinct about these things. My open admiration is always rewarded with armloads of rhubarb, clutches of lettuce, pecks of tomatoes, and bushels of cucumbers, zucchini and squash. I do adore my gardening friends.

What I really concentrate on is the lawn. There doesn't seem much point in actually planting one, because whatever is growing out there looks a lot like grass to me, so what I try to do is keep it mowed. This seems like a good idea because otherwise the groundhogs will take over entirely, and this is, after all, my yard. I bought a lawn mower. It is a used lawn mower because the season is so short that I didn't think it justified a new one. Approaching it timidly, which is my usual approach to machinery, I tried to start it. There is this rope you have to pull. After only two or three seasons, I find I am able to start it about fifty percent of the time. The grass grows a lot in the intervals between my successes.

I tried hiring a neighbor's boy to cut the lawn. Usually it rained when he was scheduled. Now and then things worked out and I had a lovely smelling, well trimmed lawn. At such times I was tempted to lavish hugs on the poor boy, but I restrained myself and merely paid him. After awhile he went off to Africa with the Peace Corps. The next fellow showed up with his own riding lawn mower. I was impressed. He buzzed around on that thing, making fine progress until he ran into my sculpture which then fell on him. He had to go and have his head stitched up, and for some reason he did not

176

offer to return. I think he was embarrassed.

This year one of my sons came over and helped me get the mower started. I mowed about half the lawn before it ran out of gas so I could come inside and take a nap. Half of the lawn looked really nice, although I noticed there was a crooked wheel on the mower. Next day I hired an ambitious girl to finish it, and she was doing really well, plowing right through that ten inch grass, until the wheel fell off. Now I'm waiting for another son to come by with his truck and take it away to be welded.

Did I tell you about my weed whacker? I bought one for all those unkempt places around the rock walls and trees and foundations. It has a gas motor, too, only this one runs on gas with some oil in it. How's that for confusing? That machine won't start for me either, even after two or three seasons. But it doesn't really matter because somebody borrowed it and I can't remember who.

So like I said, this is a steaming jungle. There are those who would advise me to let nature take its course and be at one with God's creation, but how would I locate my front door? Maybe I'll just get a machete. They're pretty straightforward.

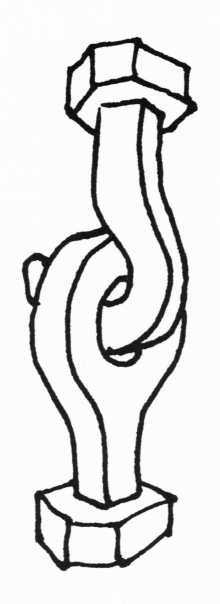

VIRTUAL IS A SEVEN LETTER DIRTY WORD

I suppose that the computer world is in about the same shape now as the world of the motor car was when they were first invented. Everybody in those days (they tell me) had to have a car, because they would get you to where you wanted to go so much faster than that old horse. But sooner or later that car would get stuck in the mud or have a flat tire, or simply refuse to go, and that old horse would be called upon to extract that nifty new car from its difficulties.

I only mention this because my frustration level is far above flood stage at this point. For Christmas I received this computer. It is a lovely computer, regardless of the fact that people chuckle at its vintage. When one of my children decided to upgrade, this whole expensive outfit was otherwise destined for destruction, I suppose. So this was seen as a marvelous opportunity to bring Mother, kicking and screaming, into the digital age.

So here it is, with all its myriad parts. There is a mother board (is that one word or two?) and a keyboard, and a printer, and a box full of discs, and a ream of paper, and even a mouse. I did mention that I really didn't think that I needed a mouse. I really don't like mice, either mechanical or furry.

There are those who are still amused about my first performance with this mechanical one, since for some reason it took both hands for me to run it. This computer sits here on the old desk where my late husband used to make his model airplanes. The desk is struggling mightily to hold all the pieces of this modern technology. Its legs are tied together with a length of old clothesline, and the keyboard is resting upon an open drawer, but so far it hasn't shown signs of collapsing. There is also an impressive collection of operating manuals, but they are all written in a foreign language.

They made me give my typewriter to my grandson who is writing a science fiction book, so I need to discover how to make this thing work. I did type and print a few letters and they didn't look too bad—even in that strange font—so I was feeling somewhat encouraged until my #3 son decided I needed access to E mail. You need to realize that I am the person who had a microwave for a year before I was able to do anything more than coffee with it. I need time to get used to things.

The whole E-mail thing came about when I wondered aloud about my sister in Anchorage. I suppose we could live farther apart than New York and Alaska, but that's the way it is. My son said, "I'll hook you up to JUNO." I pointed out that she didn't live there—it was Anchorage. He enjoyed that very much, and since he was between jobs at the time, he really did hook me up to JUNO. I should mention, for those who are as unaware as I, that JUNO is an E mail service. I also like to mention the fact that he was between jobs because I notice that every time you start any simple function with a computer, you come up for air many hours later, sometimes even having accomplished something.

So I called my sister and had a nice chat, and she gave me her E mail address. She's my younger sister. She understands these things. It only took my son two days to unravel my copy of her address and send her a note on his computer, with a copy to me. Then it only took me a day and a half to find it on my computer. That was mainly because I kept getting lost among the various programs. For quite awhile I was wandering around trying to find Carmen Sandiego. That's one of those games that the computer people invented to make sure you will sit there forever. This Sandiego person is supposed to be a bad guy and you're supposed to be a "gum shoe" and nab him—or maybe her.

Finally today I found his letter. That was impressive. I typed a quick response. Then I put it in my "out box" and typed a note to my sister. That was a mistake. For some reason, which I'm sure will only take two or three days to figure out, there was some sort of error in the transmission. Maybe it was because I typed her address the wrong way and had to do it over about six times while trying to get rid of the wrong part. It does seem to want to hang onto your mistakes and flaunt them.

It occurred to me that perhaps I could erase my sister's note and just send the other one, but that only led to another trip down the back alleys of this dark machine. Finally I gave up in disgust. It only took me fifteen minutes to disentangle myself from its clutches.

Hours later I called my son and complained bitterly about my dilemma. He enjoyed it immensely. I mentioned that if this were an early automobile, someone would have been yelling by now, "Get a horse!" He pointed out that the difference is that this is just virtual reality. No horse can rescue me. It's just as well. I am not a horse person either. The whole thing is perfectly nebulous. I am grateful for the telephone and the US mail.

Incidentally, I did actually/virtually find and arrest that Carmen Sandiego culprit. However, there doesn't seem to be any way to prosecute, or even get a pat on the back, or a virtual promotion from the rank of gumshoe.

I am virtually discouraged.

MINORITY REPORT

They're taking the census again. I vaguely remember being counted in 1960, but have no recollection of any subsequent census. Where was I in 1970, 80, and 90? Did anybody care?

The local paper says that this locality will be losing some more representation in Albany and Washington DC because everybody's gone elsewhere.

If my husband were still around he would be secretly—well, not so secretly—pleased about that. I still recall 1969 when we moved to that remote hillside with the expansive view. Every night we had enjoyed the sight of the seven streetlights in the town of Adirondack, miles away on the other side of Schroon Lake. As spring arrived, other lights began to appear here and there in the distance. He would gaze out upon this misty sight and then turn to me and say, "You know, it's getting awfully crowded around here."

If it hadn't been for his wife and seven children, he'd have made a really great hermit.

All right, I know the north country is not the most convenient place for permanent habitation. I still remember, with some amazement, the first winter I spent here fifty years ago.

My father, back there in Seattle, would see in his newspaper pictures of Buffalo under all that snow, and he'd write and tell me, "If you can get word out, I'll send in a helicopter for you." He had already pointed out that not even the Indians ever lived in the Adirondacks in the winter.

It seems to me, though, that there is some sort of inequity at work. Here we are in the midst of all this wilderness, and we have to be represented in state and national government by people we don't even know. People, I might add, who don't know us. How can a representative from someplace like Plattsburgh or Glens Falls have any concept about our wants or needs? Why should that representative even care, since we represent so few votes?

Now, occasionally we will be observed—even noticed—by a sojourner from the more populated part of New York State. (That would include most everybody else from Buffalo to Albany and New York City to Plattsburgh.) Since these parts are no longer referred to as a "howling wilderness" it has gained a reputation as a place of "rustic beauty," a "sportsman's paradise," and a place where one might go to renew one's spirit, indulge in recreation and get away from it all. Such glowing phrases do appear every so often in various publications, whenever the region is "discovered" by yet another correspondent. Which is amazingly often.

As a result of this periodic discovery, local resorts and real estate dealers will be entertaining the curious, and there will be those who will find that there are distractions to this idyllic scene. Some of them will be so disappointed as to feel compelled to voice their concerns to a local paper via a letter to the editor.

They will decry the lack of a sense of order to the local landscape. They will mention unpainted houses, porches full of discarded machinery and yards strewn with old abandoned vehicles. They will ask why the locals don't clean up their act, instead of besmirching nature's glory. They might even go so far as to say that we who live here don't appreciate what we have. One could almost imagine that the local population is a detriment to their enjoyment of "their" Adirondack Park.

So I would like to extend a few words of explanation, not to be confused with apology.

To begin with, one cannot eat the scenery. That does not mean that those who live in the midst of it do not appreciate it. For most of us, that's why we live here. But one must have a source of income. This region has the highest unemployment figures in the state. Retirement incomes keep a lot of us going. For the rest there is not a lot of opportunity. Also, living costs are high, because of the cold, and the isolation. If one is employed during the summer, one might conceivably receive unemployment insurance in the "off" season, but you need to make sure you have made yourself eligible with enough weeks of employment. Also, the office to which you must report is usually forty or fifty miles away, so be sure to have a car, and save money for gas, and pray that the roads are passable when you have to report. The rules are the same for any other services you might need. And don't expect the people in charge of such things to be courteous. They have their suspicions.

If any of your family needs a doctor, then you are in big trouble, because you can't afford health insurance. So you also pray for good health. The stuff on your porch is your version of the "culch pile" of frugal New Englanders. Somebody gave you their old washing machine, and when it quit, you stored it under any available roof in case you need parts for the next one. Besides, you can't take it to the dump. You don't have a truck, or maybe tires, and there is a fee to pay there that you also don't have. Same is true of those old cars out in the "dooryard."

If you were born into one of the old families, you probably live in the old farmhouse, and the land got divvied up when the folks died. You have trouble making the tax payments, because land values keep rising and you can't do anything about that. Your education was over when/if you finished high school because you couldn't afford college, and had to go to work to pay for your board. School taxes are bad because the state keeps requiring a lot of things you can see no need for, and teachers get a lot more money than you ever will, and you kind of wonder why, since anybody can see you're working harder than they are. And then the state comes and buys more property and tears down any buildings so it can be forever wild, and then pays minimum taxes because it's just unimproved land and your taxes go up again.

So they're taking the census again. I sure hope they can find everybody around here, especially the ones out at the ends of the dirt roads in their make-do housing. I hope the census taker doesn't get stuck. I hope everybody gets counted. We need all the people we can find.

Are You Paying Attention?

These last few years, my summer job has been taking care of reservations and checking in campers at a nearby family campground. This pays nicely for all the trouble I get into the rest of the year. I try to keep everybody happy, and avoid putting two campers into one space at the same time. In order to do this, I use a computer, and enjoy seeing the look of mild surprise when people check in and discover technology in the back woods. I don't mention that during the winter I am computer illiterate. Well, maybe not completely illiterate, but certainly not fluent. Also, I have learned that murmuring "Oh, oh" during the transaction destroys my credibility, so I try to avoid that.

Every now and then, the campground loses electric power, and it's back to old-fashioned methods. When this happens, I dig out the old forms, look the customer straight in the eye, and say, "All I need is your signature, the number of adults in your party, and your license plate number. I already have your other information." They look back at me very intelligently, and then fill out the entire form: address, equipment—all that. I have learned not to interrupt.

Ninety five percent of our campers also never read the

fine print on the registration that they sign. There are lots of things there about how the management is not responsible, and reserves the right, and so on. Now and then someone reads it, and I am always surprised. Sometimes they just ask, "What's this?" I tell them they are merely signing away their first-born. So far, no one has believed me.

Nobody ever reads the signs at our beach, either, and I can't say that I blame them. The health department requires a plethora of rules and regulations, and the insurance company has added details. As the resident sign painter, I can tell you it's pretty boring.

Maybe that's why nobody ever pays any attention. We're all on overload.

Or maybe we simply choose not to pay attention. Like the people with dogs who decide you really don't mean that their particularly charming pet needs to be on a leash, because their dog never makes any trouble. And then there are the signs that say the speed limit is 10 mph. When one is in a tearing rush to get to one's campsite and start unwinding, ten miles per hour seems a bit unreasonable, I suppose.

However, I may have discovered at least a partial solution.

One dark night, this past summer, some of our more adventurous young campers decided to ignore our prominently posted rules about the eleven o'clock curfew. They went down to the beach and carried off our signs clearly stating such things as, "Life Guard on duty, 11 a.m. to 5 p.m." and

"No Lifeguard, Swimming Prohibited".

While we looked diligently for the missing signs, I hastily printed substitutes, since the health department would not permit use of the beach without them. I used a large magic marker on some foam board. In my haste, I inadvertently left out a few letters. We wound up with signs saying, "Life Guad on duty", and, "Swiming Prohibited". The weather was hot and sunny. The swimmers were poised for action. I discovered my mistakes just as the signs were snatched up and installed in great haste at the beach. I tried to snatch them back. I said, "Hey, let me just insert a few missing letters." They said, "Aw, don't be so picky. They'll do."

I considered running after them, wielding my magic marker, but it occurred to me that it would entail a sizeable loss of dignity. Besides, the telephone might ring. My motto has always been, never leave a ringing phone unanswered.

Well. There went my reputation as a professional sign painter. I was the recipient of derision and the butt of jokes for days. When the original signs were finally located and returned, my sorry substitutes were in great demand as souvenirs.

But. They paid attention!

Now, everyone is well aware of the beach rules. I'm thinking maybe I should do a lot of new signs. Maybe they could say, "spud limit, 10K". Do you think there'd be some discussion? Maybe we could say, "All dogs must be lashed."

What do you think?

NOWHERE

It is time to apologize to Ohio and Iowa. I always get them mixed up. They sound so much alike, and I'm not too clear about where they are. Somewhere west of the east coast and east of the west coast, south of Canada and north of that old Mason-Dixon Line, I reckon. I need to apologize because these are places where real people live, and as a fellow American I ought to get it straight.

My situation is somewhat similar. I live in the Adirondacks. If I venture to New York City and am asked, "Where are you from?" I might say "upstate." That doesn't do much good. To a New York City dweller, upstate is Westchester and points north and west. They will ask, "Albany? Rochester, Buffalo, Syracuse?" I reply, "No, the mountains." They will say, "Oh, Sullivan County?" "No," I will say, "not the Catskills; farther north. The Adirondacks." Slowly the dawn will rise in their minds and their eyes will light up. "Oh, Lake George," they'll say, or maybe, "Oh, Lake Placid!" Quite often I settle for that.

I once served time at a camping show in Boston, promoting Adirondack campgrounds. People would stop by and inquire where the Adirondacks were. One Bostonian wondered whether that was in northern Massachusetts. I'm not entirely convinced that there is a northern Massachusetts.

Possibly one needs to be understanding when people from other states are not well acquainted with New York State geography, although Massachusetts is not all that far away. However, one ought to be able to expect that fellow New Yorkers might have some familiarity with the Adirondacks.

It is understandable that New York City inhabitants might have trouble visualizing anything other than a city land-scape. However, is it too much to ask that the millions of New York State inhabitants who do not dwell in the shadow of those skyscrapers have some idea of what the rest of their state is like?

Not only do I live in the Adirondacks, but also I live in a little village called Olmstedville. Are you having any trouble with that? Olmstedville is a part of the township of Minerva. Does that help? If you go up the Northway to Exit 26, get off there and then turn left at the Wells House in Pottersville, and drive six miles west, you'll actually be in Olmstedville. At least for a minute or two.

There is actually a school in Olmstedville, called Minerva Central School. We have about one hundred fifty students. It is not the smallest school around. Twenty miles northwest of us is Newcomb Central School. These schools get together to field a very sharp basketball team. I have a grandson at Newcomb who is graduating in a class of three. He was half of the class until another girl moved to town.

Now I don't know whether he will be the salutatorian, the valedictorian, or the lowest ranking member of his class.

When people from these parts journey to the "big city," it's apt to be Glens Falls. Although Glens Falls is five miles south of the official Adirondack Park, Adirondack Community College is located there. In spite of that, it's a nice little city, where people are usually polite, even though some of them have never heard of Olmstedville. Whenever I go there, I can get radio stations on my car radio that don't make it to where I live. One winter afternoon, I was departing Glens Falls for home, into the teeth of a blizzard. I recall tuning in to an Albany station to get the weather report. The announcer said, "The weather looks good. All roads are clear and there is no snow in the forecast. Thruway conditions are excellent." I wondered rather bitterly what planet he occupied. However, this was not unusual for Albany stations, who remain mostly clueless about us. I should probably mention that Albany stations do give the weather in the summer months, as far north as Lake George. They might even say a few words about Lake Placid. Those of us who live in that nether world in between apparently do not have any weather.

I listened one evening to a commentator discussing Teddy Roosevelt's sojourn in the Adirondacks. He told of his midnight ride to the train station in Elizabethtown, of all places, to assume the presidency when McKinley died. I was so incensed I nearly ran off the road. There has never been a train station in Elizabethtown. North Creek has been celebrating for years that midnight ride to their train station.

I'm not sure why it is that people get so mixed up about the Adirondacks. Maybe it's because the Adirondack Park is so big, and there are so few people actually living here. And of course there are not that many of us who actually mind what anybody thinks one way or the other. It's something like the fisherman who has a favorite fishing hole and he's not about to let on where that is.

We lived for awhile, here, high up on the side of a hill overlooking a large lake. In the winter we could gaze across that lake and see about seven little lights on the other side. In the spring, the number of lights would begin to increase until they dotted the entire shore. My husband, the original Adirondack hermit type, would turn to me and say, "Y'know, it's getting awfully crowded around here."

One of my sons lives in Indian Lake. He says if the Adirondacks is "nowhere," then he lives in the middle of nowhere. He likes that. He likes to tell people he's from the Adirondacks, then pause, and then ask, "Do you know where that is?" If they say, "No." he replies, "Good." It may be that the folks in Ohio and Iowa feel this way, too. We won't even mention Idaho.

BOTHERATION

You are cordially invited to the big party I'm having to celebrate the completion of my garage. Maybe that word, garage, should be capitalized, bold face, underlined. You may recall that where I come from the normal state of affairs is that there is always a garage for the car. I can remember some people we knew there who never even would take their car out in the rain. Of course, I can also remember when the speed limit was thirty-five miles an hour, and gas was twenty-nine cents a gallon. Maybe I should just skip that part.

When I moved into this little early Adirondack farm-house, about twenty years ago, I really didn't give much thought to a garage. I hadn't had one since 1969, and other concerns loomed larger. Howsomever, I really have become less and less inclined to want to go out the door on a cold morning and shovel a path to the car, pry open a frozen door, dust out the snow that blows in, dig around for the scraper, scrape the windshield, brush off the hood, and dig a channel around the whole vehicle preparatory to facing the challenge of plowing out of the driveway in second gear while praying that there is not any oncoming traffic, because if I need to stop, the likelihood of gaining enough momentum to try again is practically nonexistent. If that last sentence seems a little long and tedious, then I have created the right atmosphere.

So I saved up the salary from my summer job for the last five years or so, and declined the trip to Northern Italy that my friends are taking, and decided that this is the year for building that garage. Not only that, but also I need a back door, a back porch and a covered walkway. Otherwise, in order to use that garage I would need to go out the front door and shovel a path all the way around the house to it.

Although I don't often indulge in a lot of planning, I actually worked out all these details, complete with floor plans, last spring, while I waited for things to thaw out. That was when I realized that I'd need a new mortgage. Off I went to our friendly neighborhood bank and applied for one. I filled out reams of forms, entertained the appraisers, and waited for wonderful things to happen. I can hardly remember a time when I didn't have a mortgage to pay, so I didn't give it a whole lot of thought.

One day I got a call from the friendly neighborhood banker.

"Mrs. Gregson," she said, "We find that on your limited income, the payments on a fifteen year mortgage would be too high."

She paused.

I waited.

"So we have decided to give you a thirty year mortgage."

After I got through laughing, I said, "Do you know how old I'll be in thirty years?"

I could tell, however, that they'd thought about that. It was obvious that they weren't worried about getting their money back. So I said fine, whatever. That's just another item for my heirs to work out.

By the time it was black fly season, I had notified my various builder sons that I had funding and I had plans and it was time to put me on their work lists.

My #5 son said, "Do you have a building permit?"

I went to the town office and got the application. The following day I called the building inspector and asked how to fill it out. There were terms and specifications that meant nothing to my muddled brain. He said, "Just sign where it says, 'owner,' write a check for the proper amount, and send it to me." Two days later I had a building permit. I noticed that it would be good for two years. I thought about that. Then I called #5 son and told him yes, I had a permit.

Nothing happened.

I should explain that between the five of them, my sons have the expertise to do any building job that my mind can conjure up. Their father had been like that. I only had to wave my arms around, draw a few pictures, and if I could keep him interested long enough, his interpretation of my dream would become a reality. So I was conditioned to expect something similar. It turned out, however, that though I was certainly on their lists, there were numerous others that were on those lists ahead of me.

Also, there were two conditions that were not in my favor. One was sibling rivalry. No matter what one son did for me, another son would inevitably appear and ask, "Why'd you do it that way?"

There is also the problem with payment. They wouldn't dream of charging their mother what they charge everybody else for their work. It just wouldn't be right. So they really can't afford to work for me. Even though I have all this money.

So I waited. Along about August, I visited my #1 son at his job site and asked whether he could recommend someone to do this garage project. I really do prefer his carpentry, and his ideas on finishing are always better than mine, but time was running out. It must be that I struck a cord.

Suddenly there were stakes and strings and little red flags appearing out there. Presently I was watching fill being brought in and graded. Soon there was a cement slab, and then the walls began to rise. People began to stop me in the grocery store and post office to exclaim about my new garage. The roof went on, and I was busily dipping shingles in stain and hanging them on the clothesline to dry for the walls, while #3 son was installing electricity

Then one day nobody came. Pretty soon I found a note that said they'd be back in a week or so. After awhile I ran out of boxes in which to store the stained shingles.

And then it snowed. I went out and shoveled a path to

my car, pried open the door, dusted off the snow that blew in, found the scraper, scraped the windshield, brushed off the hood, etc., etc. Now I'm sitting here looking out at my garage-in-progress and wondering whether I should maybe go to Northern Italy.

But stand by. You won't want to miss that party.

— Party Time —

Continuity

Once upon a time -. Well, no, it was actually September, 1952. We were on our way home from the hospital in Ticonderoga with the new baby. Greg and his father had come to fetch us. We had to use his father's car because our old '39 Ford pickup truck was temporarily incapacitated. So we stopped in Schroon Lake so that Mr. Gregson could bid in a few things at the auction.

My father-in-law was addicted to auctions, and this was a big one. It was the estate of the Miller sisters who had inherited the Revere Ware Company, and it was extensive. There was a large rustic mansion, on top of a secluded hill, called Tip Top; its gate house, down on the highway; a spacious inn, located at Schroon Falls, called The Big Tavern; and a smaller one across the road from it known as The Little Tavern. There was also a hunting lodge, three miles out into the woods, called Manawakee; and an old schoolhouse. All these places were full of furniture, books and supplies.

Among other things, Mr. Gregson acquired a moose head, two living room chairs, various braided rugs, the hunting lodge and the schoolhouse.

Manawakee was a fascinating place, and apparently

dated back to around the time of prohibition. The main building was built of logs, with little secret compartments just the right size for bottles of booze. I was told that one of the garages had been occupied by an old bullet-riddled car. Apparently someone else had acquired the car. One small cabin was equipped with a bar, and decorated with old crows and four roses. There were two outhouses; one was identified by an oil painting of a pointer, the other had a painting of a setter.

The great room had a big boulder rising through the floor and used as part of the décor. One end was entirely occupied by a huge stone fireplace and a built in cauldron, certainly large enough to have served as the official oversized hot water heater.

On either side of the fireplace were two couches, with high Victorian back, built of genuine porcupine chewed oak, and covered with ugly brown plush. They were each nine feet long. I fell in love with those two couches.

Greg and his father ran hunting lodges in at Manawakee for two or three seasons, and then it was sold to a writer who wanted solitude. The couches were transported to the basement of a motel that Greg's cousin had built in Schroon Lake. They needed lots of room, and this basement had it. There were ping-pong tables and a pool table down there. The couches languished there until 1969.

That was the year when we returned to the Adirondacks after six years of fruitless wandering. We bought one hundred acres from that cousin, up on the side of a hill overlooking Schroon Lake. The Northway had been built while we were away, and Greg had decided that campers would be arriving in large numbers needing the great campground that he was going to build.

The barn that we moved into had very little furnishings, and we hadn't brought much with us. Also it was big. There was, of course, that ugly old barber chair sitting there enjoying the view. I was the only one who thought it was ugly, and I was determined to be rid of it. I remembered those two couches in Bob's basement, and knowing how Bob loved that old barber chair, I proposed a swap. Finally those couches were mine!

The couches went through many changes. We had a long history together. I recovered them at least three times over the years, mainly because I was too cheap to buy sturdy upholstery material. When I moved to my present small home, there was room for just one of them. The other one stayed behind and eventually wound up with my youngest son.

There was just one wall in my little living room that could accommodate that nine-foot couch, so we brought it in the front door and put it there. Then, when its most recent cover began to fray, I decided it was time to have that couch refinished, rebuilt, and covered with a good quality upholstery. And this time I would have it done professionally. Since I had become a real art teacher, I was gaining a new respect for professionalism. So I sent it out to be operated upon, and acquired an old wicker couch from another friend to use in the interim. I knew it would take a long time for all those professionals to do their things.

Some time during the absence of that big couch, I prevailed upon my sons to build a fireplace where the front door had been. My house is located very near to the busy road, and the front door had opened right into that noise and confusion. We moved it to the side, right opposite the stairway landing.

The various operations on the old couch, true to Adirondack tradition, took two or three years. When it was finally ready to return to my living room, we made an interesting discovery. We could not get it into the new door, past the stairway landing and into the living room. We tried various maneuvers. We tried tipping it up, and we tried all sorts of odd angles. We tried backing it into the kitchen. There was no way. Finally we did the only possible thing. We took it up those stairs and parked it in my studio, directly above the place where it belonged in the living room.

Probably I should draw you a diagram. There it has rested for these last few years, just waiting for an opportunity to return to its rightful place.

Finally I have a plan. My boys are finally building a garage for the car. Revolutionary! After that, they're going to have to build a back porch with a back door so I can get to the garage without having to walk all the way around the house. When I've acquired a back door, then we can bring that couch down the stairs, out the front door, around to the back porch, into the back door, through the kitchen, and finally into the living room.

Aren't you glad you're not one of my children? They don't get much time off. If all goes well, some day one of them will acquire this old couch and rescue the other one and reunite them somewhere. I will smile at them from my grave.